KOREN SHADMI

The TWILIGHT MAN

Rod Serling and the Birth of Television

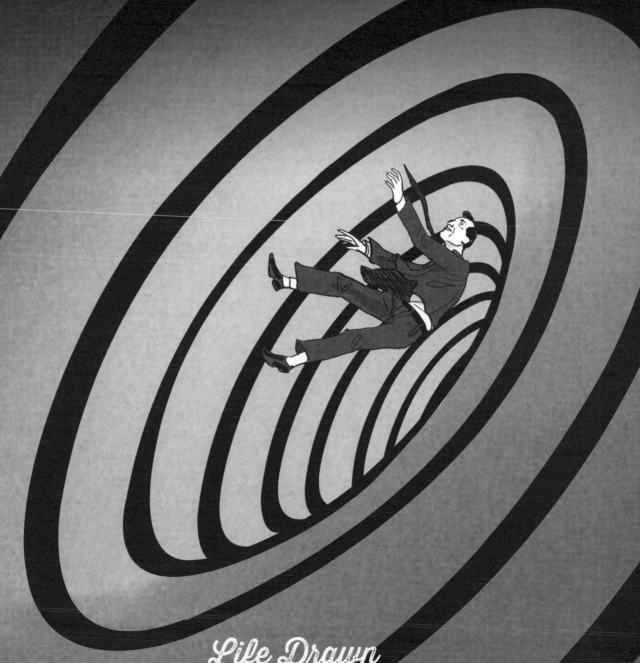

Life Drawn

Koren Shadmi
Story & Art

•

AndWorld Design
Letterer

•

Fabrice Sapolsky
Editor

Amanda Lucido
Assistant Editor

Jerry Frissen
Senior Art Director

Fabrice Giger
Publisher

Rights and Licensing - licensing@humanoids.com
Press and Social Media - pr@humanoids.com

Dedicated to Aviv Shadmi.

The author would like to thank
Mary Abramson, Arlen Schumer,
Ido Fluk and Yaron Kaver.

THE TWILIGHT MAN

PART I

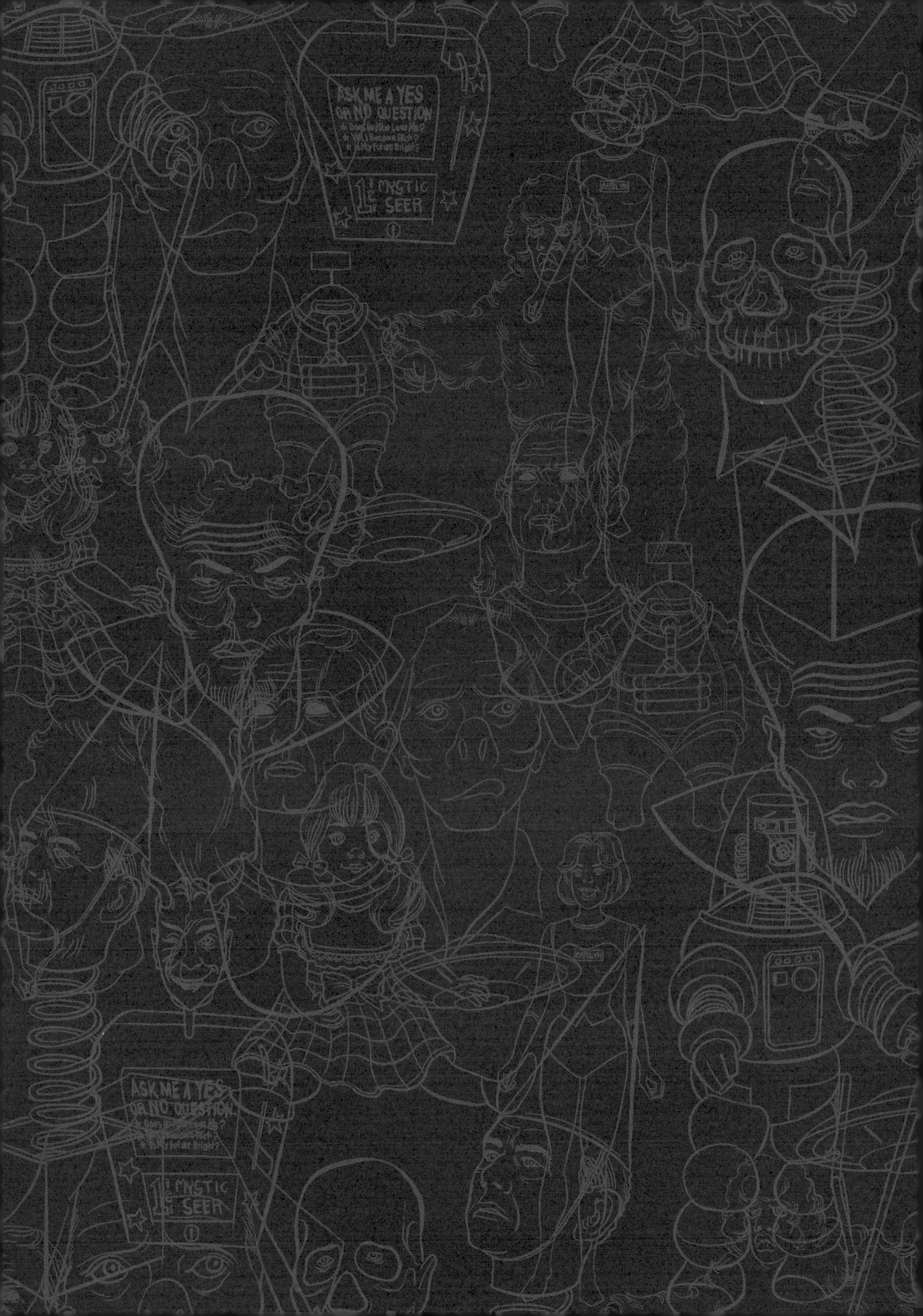
ASK ME A YES OR NO QUESTION
MYSTIC SEER
ASK ME A YES OR NO QUESTION
MYSTIC SEER

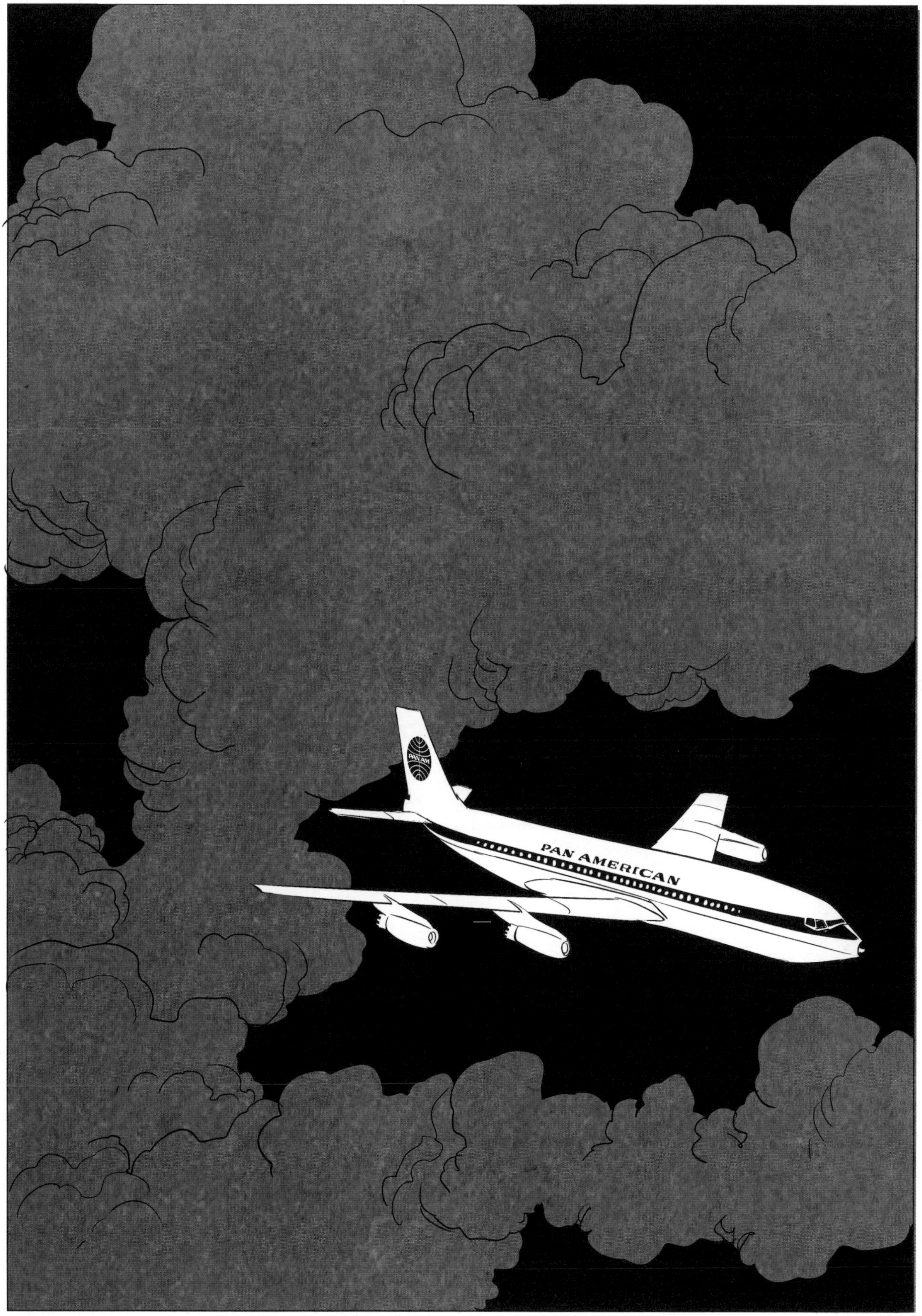
PAN AM
PAN AMERICAN

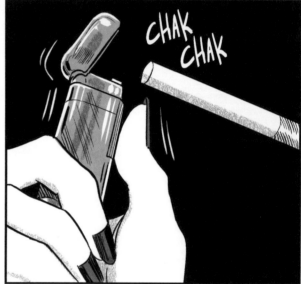

CHAK
CHAK

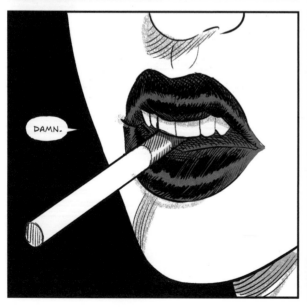

DAMN.

CHAK!

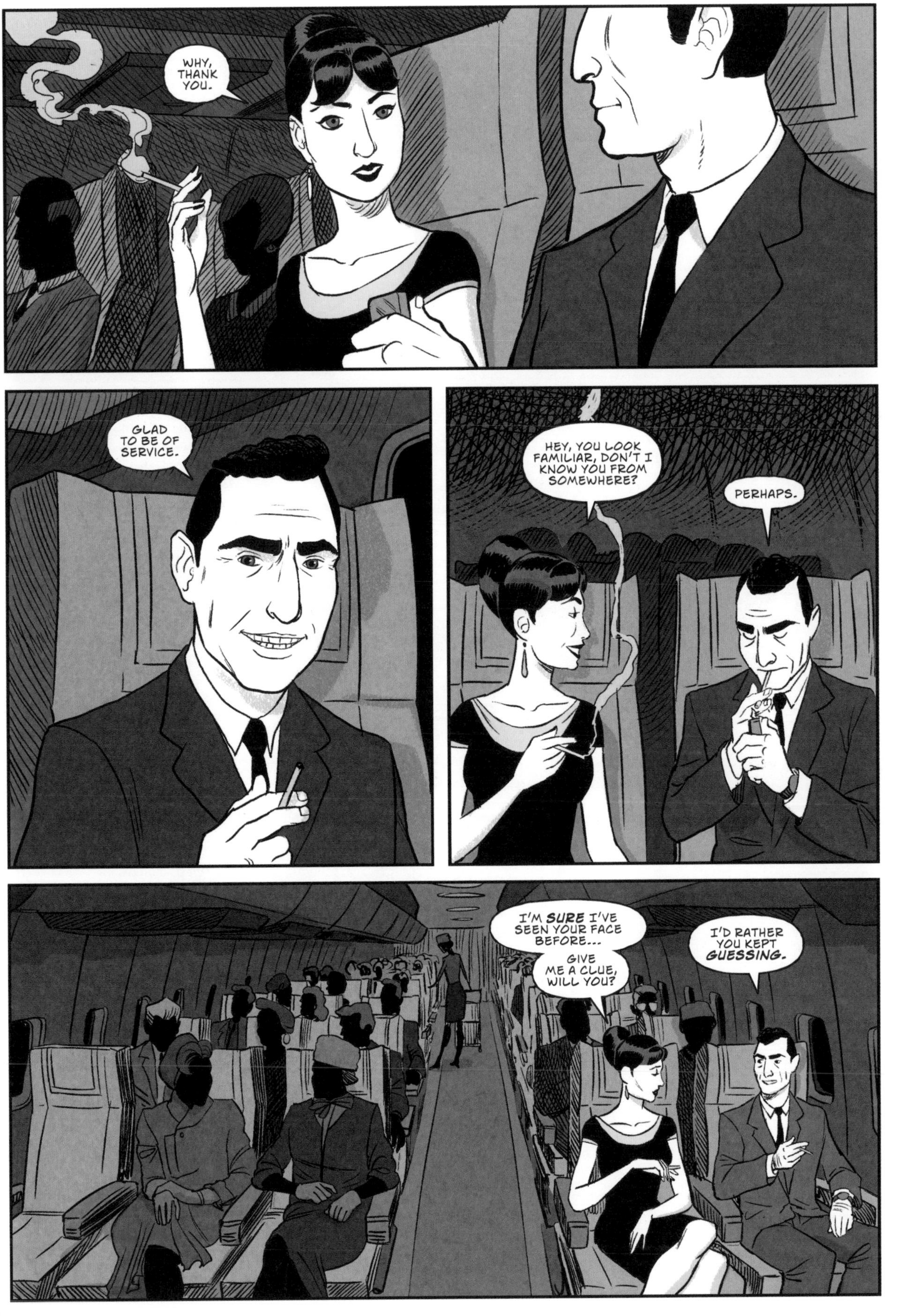
WHY, THANK YOU.
GLAD TO BE OF SERVICE.
HEY, YOU LOOK FAMILIAR, DON'T I KNOW YOU FROM SOMEWHERE?
PERHAPS.
I'M **SURE** I'VE SEEN YOUR FACE BEFORE...
GIVE ME A CLUE, WILL YOU?
I'D RATHER YOU KEPT **GUESSING.**

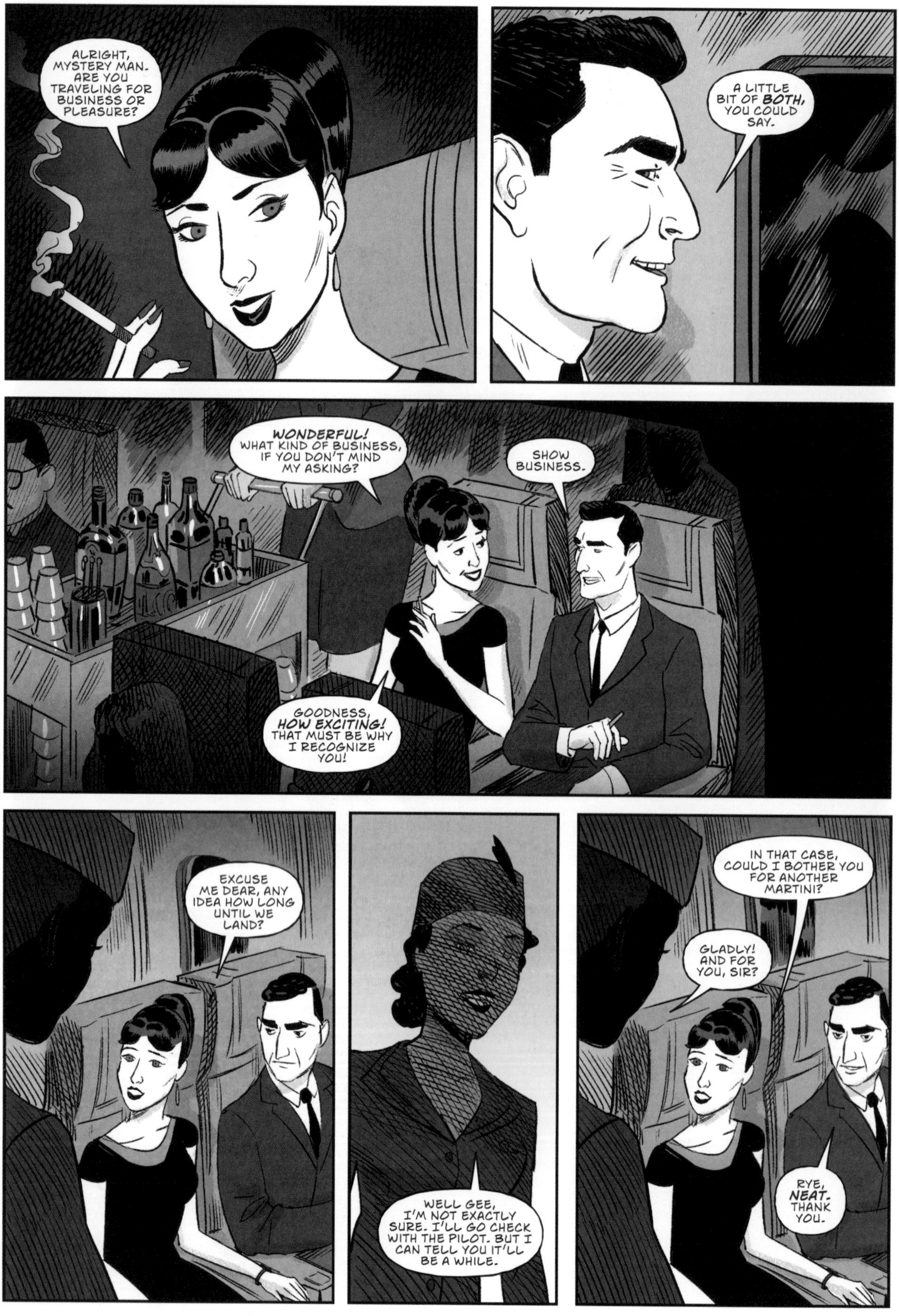
ALRIGHT, MYSTERY MAN. ARE YOU TRAVELING FOR BUSINESS OR PLEASURE?
A LITTLE BIT OF BOTH, YOU COULD SAY.
WONDERFUL! WHAT KIND OF BUSINESS, IF YOU DON'T MIND MY ASKING?
SHOW BUSINESS.
GOODNESS, HOW EXCITING! THAT MUST BE WHY I RECOGNIZE YOU!
EXCUSE ME DEAR, ANY IDEA HOW LONG UNTIL WE LAND?
WELL GEE, I'M NOT EXACTLY SURE. I'LL GO CHECK WITH THE PILOT. BUT I CAN TELL YOU IT'LL BE A WHILE.
IN THAT CASE, COULD I BOTHER YOU FOR ANOTHER MARTINI?
GLADLY! AND FOR YOU, SIR?
RYE, NEAT. THANK YOU.

IT FEELS AS THOUGH THIS FLIGHT MIGHT LAST FOREVER...

TIME CAN BE *DECEITFUL* WHEN YOU'RE UP IN THE STRATOSPHERE.

YOU KNOW, I'M REALLY IN A *RUT.*

WHAT SEEMS TO BE THE TROUBLE?

I JUST CAN'T MANAGE TO FALL ASLEEP.

AND AS IF THAT'S NOT ENOUGH, I FORGOT TO BRING A BOOK. I'VE ALREADY READ THE IN-FLIGHT MAGAZINE TWICE OVER.

THAT'S QUITE A PREDICAMENT YOU'RE IN. I USUALLY BRING A BOOK MYSELF, OR AT LEAST A NOTEPAD. BUT IT SEEMS I'VE FORGOTTEN BOTH THIS TIME AROUND.

IT LOOKS LIKE WE ARE BOTH *DOOMED* TO BOREDOM.

OR PERHAPS...

PERHAPS?

PERHAPS YOU COULD DAZZLE US BOTH WITH TALES FROM THE GLAMOROUS WORLD OF SHOWBIZ?

YOU MUST HAVE SOME *GREAT* STORIES!

OH, I DON'T KNOW ABOUT THAT.

COME ON! WE HAVE SO MUCH TIME TO KILL.

I'M A GREAT LISTENER.

WHY *FOUL UP* THE ATMOSPHERE WITH TALK OF TINSELTOWN?

WELL, THEN MAYBE NOT SHOWBIZ. TELL ME A STORY ABOUT SOMETHING ELSE.

HOW ABOUT THE WAR?

HOW'D YOU KNOW I WENT TO WAR?

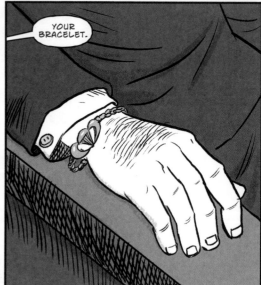

YOUR BRACELET.

TOUCHÉ! YOU HAVE A KEEN EYE. I SUPPOSE I MUST TELL MY TALE, OR ELSE...

OR ELSE!

VERY WELL THEN. LET'S SEE IF THIS OLD TIMER CAN STILL WEAVE A GOOD YARN.

THE YEAR: *1943.* THE PLACE: *CAMP TACCOA, GEORGIA.*

GATHERED HERE ARE A GROUP OF BOYS WHO *THINK* THEY ARE MEN.

THEY ARE ABOUT TO EMBARK ON A *RIGOROUS* JOURNEY--A TRUE TEST OF BODY AND SPIRIT. THOSE WHO MAKE THE CUT WILL BECOME PART OF THE NEWLY FORMED *511TH PARACHUTE INFANTRY REGIMENT.*

THESE BOYS ARE, FOR THE MOST PART, ENTHRALLED BY THE PROSPECT OF FIGHTING FOR THEIR BELOVED HOMELAND.

THEY HAVEN'T A *CLUE* OF THE GRIM FUTURE THAT AWAITS THEM IN BATTLE.

THIS PARTICULAR SPECIMEN IS *PRIVATE RODMAN SERLING.* AGE EIGHTEEN.

A JEWISH BOY FROM SMALL TOWN BINGHAMTON, NEW YORK.

HE'S HELL-BENT ON BECOMING A PARATROOPER.

AT EASE, PRIVATE. TAKE A SEAT.

SIR, YES, SIR.

I'M GOING TO MAKE IT BRIEF. I'VE GOT A LINE OF MEN FROM HERE TO SAVANNAH WANTING TO BECOME PARATROOPERS. SO, TELL ME, PRIVATE, WHY SHOULD I PICK *YOU?*

SIR, BECAUSE I WANT TO TRAIN WITH THE VERY BEST, SIR.

HRM-MMM.

ALRIGHT, KEEP 'EM COMIN'!

LATER.

I WASN'T ACCEPTED. I WAS *TOO SHORT*. SUB-REGULATION FOR A PARATROOPER.

BUT I WOULDN'T GIVE UP SO EASILY.

I RETURNED TO THE COLONEL'S OFFICE AND PLEADED MY CASE AGAIN.

ONCE MORE, HE SAID "NO."

BUT I PERSISTED.

HUH?

WHAT'S *HE* STILL DOING HERE?

SIR!

HE WON'T BUDGE. HE'S BEEN SITTING HERE FOR *HOURS*.

BOY, I TOLD YOU, THERE'RE *PLENTY* OF OTHER REGIMENTS WHO COULD USE A MOTIVATED YOUNG MAN LIKE YOURSELF.

SIR. THERE'S ONLY ONE PLACE FOR ME. I'M A PARATROOPER AT HEART. I'M NOT LEAVING 'TIL I'M ACCEPTED.

VERY WELL BOY, *YOU'RE* IN.

BUT THE ODDS ARE STILL STACKED AGAINST YOU.

MOST MEN DON'T MAKE IT. REPORT TO SERGEANT BRIGGS AT 0200.

DISMISSED.

COLONEL HOGAN WASN'T LYING.

THEY PUSHED US TO OUR *LIMITS.*

IT SEEMED AS IF EVERY DAY THERE WERE LESS OF US ON THE FIELD.

FAILING WAS OUT OF THE QUESTION. SO I KEPT AT IT.

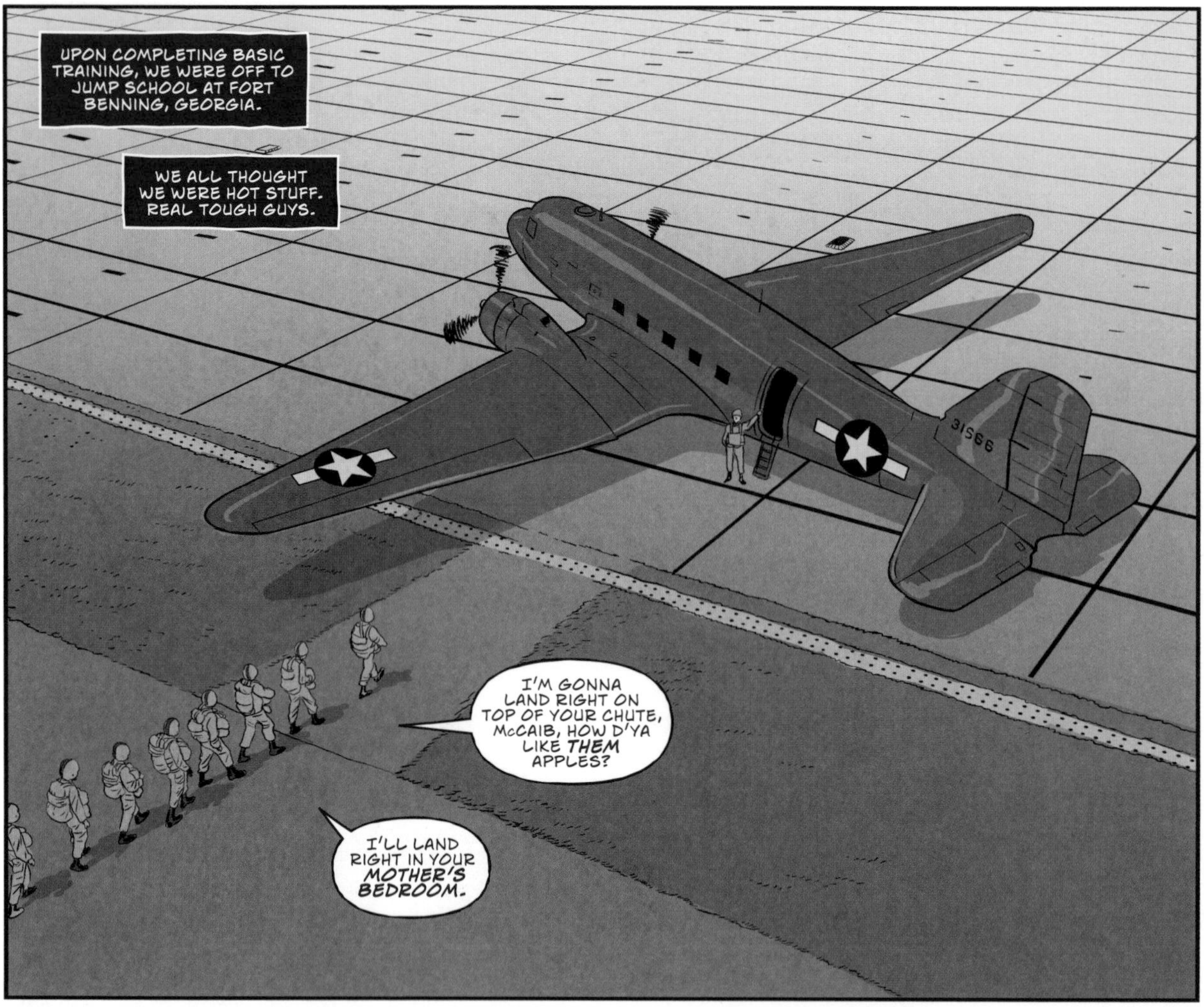
UPON COMPLETING BASIC TRAINING, WE WERE OFF TO JUMP SCHOOL AT FORT BENNING, GEORGIA.
WE ALL THOUGHT WE WERE HOT STUFF. REAL TOUGH GUYS.
31566
I'M GONNA LAND RIGHT ON TOP OF YOUR CHUTE, McCAIB, HOW D'YA LIKE THEM APPLES?
I'LL LAND RIGHT IN YOUR MOTHER'S BEDROOM.

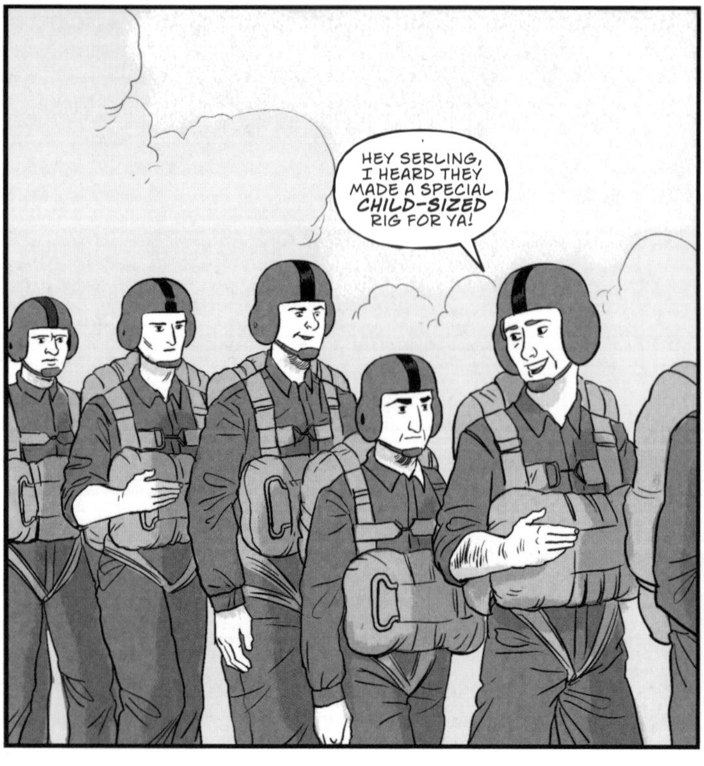
HEY SERLING, I HEARD THEY MADE A SPECIAL CHILD-SIZED RIG FOR YA!

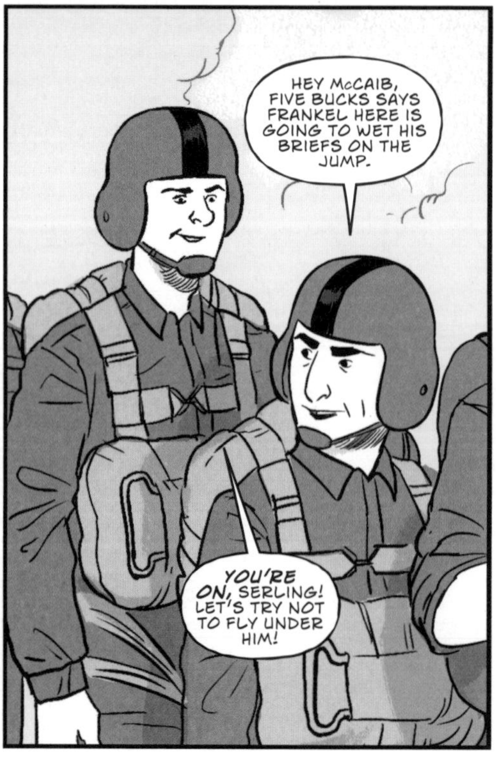
HEY McCAIB, FIVE BUCKS SAYS FRANKEL HERE IS GOING TO WET HIS BRIEFS ON THE JUMP.
YOU'RE ON, SERLING! LET'S TRY NOT TO FLY UNDER HIM!

YOU SONS O' BITCHES!

CHEER UP FRANKEL, IT'S GONNA BE A *HOOT!*

OUR TENACITY *EVAPORATED* THE MOMENT WE WERE UP IN THE AIR.

NO ONE SPOKE *A WORD.*

WE JUST SAT THERE, DROWNING IN THE ROAR OF THE ENGINES.

THE FEAR WAS *PALPABLE.*

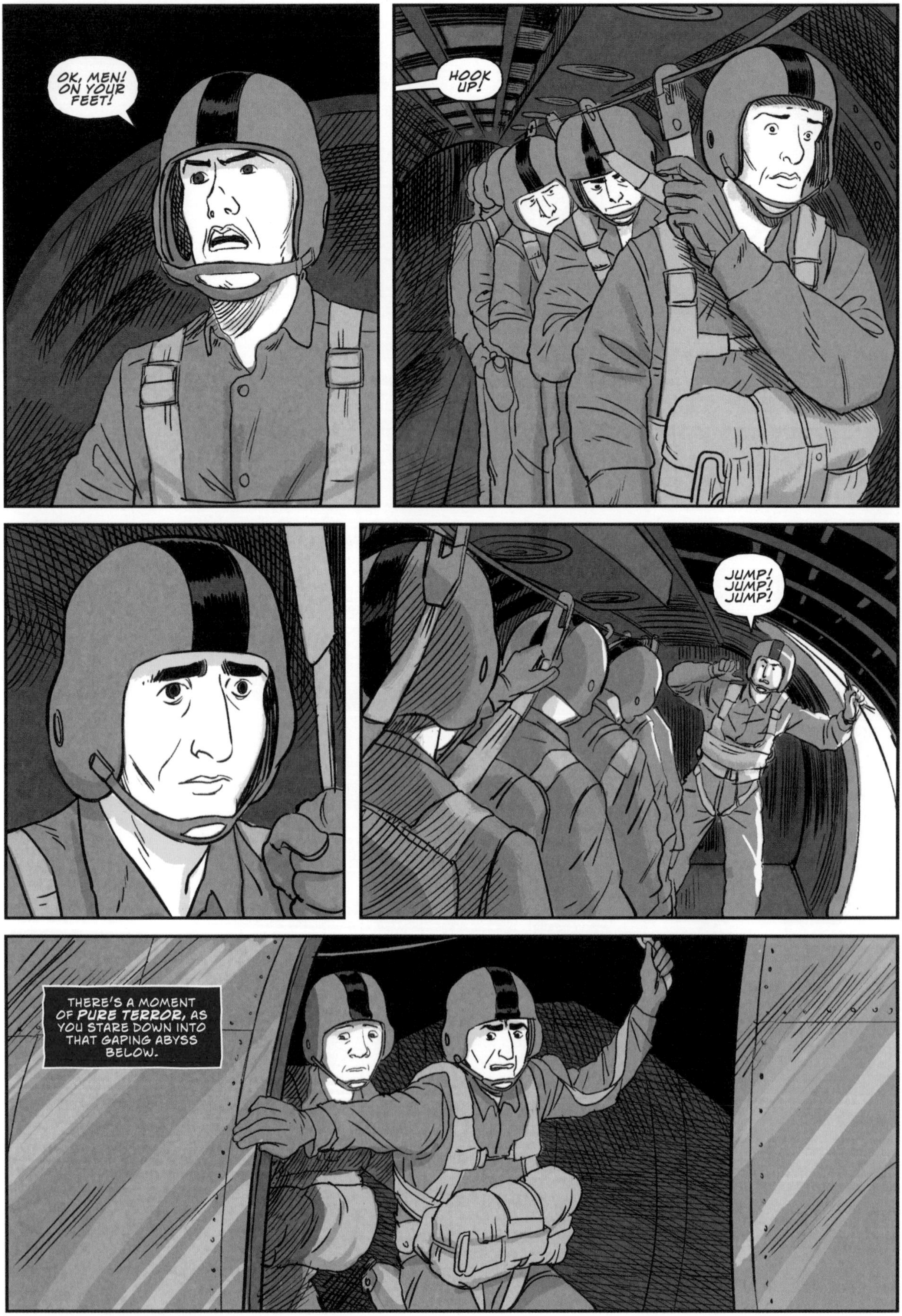
OK, MEN! ON YOUR FEET!
HOOK UP!
JUMP! JUMP! JUMP!
THERE'S A MOMENT OF PURE TERROR, AS YOU STARE DOWN INTO THAT GAPING ABYSS BELOW.

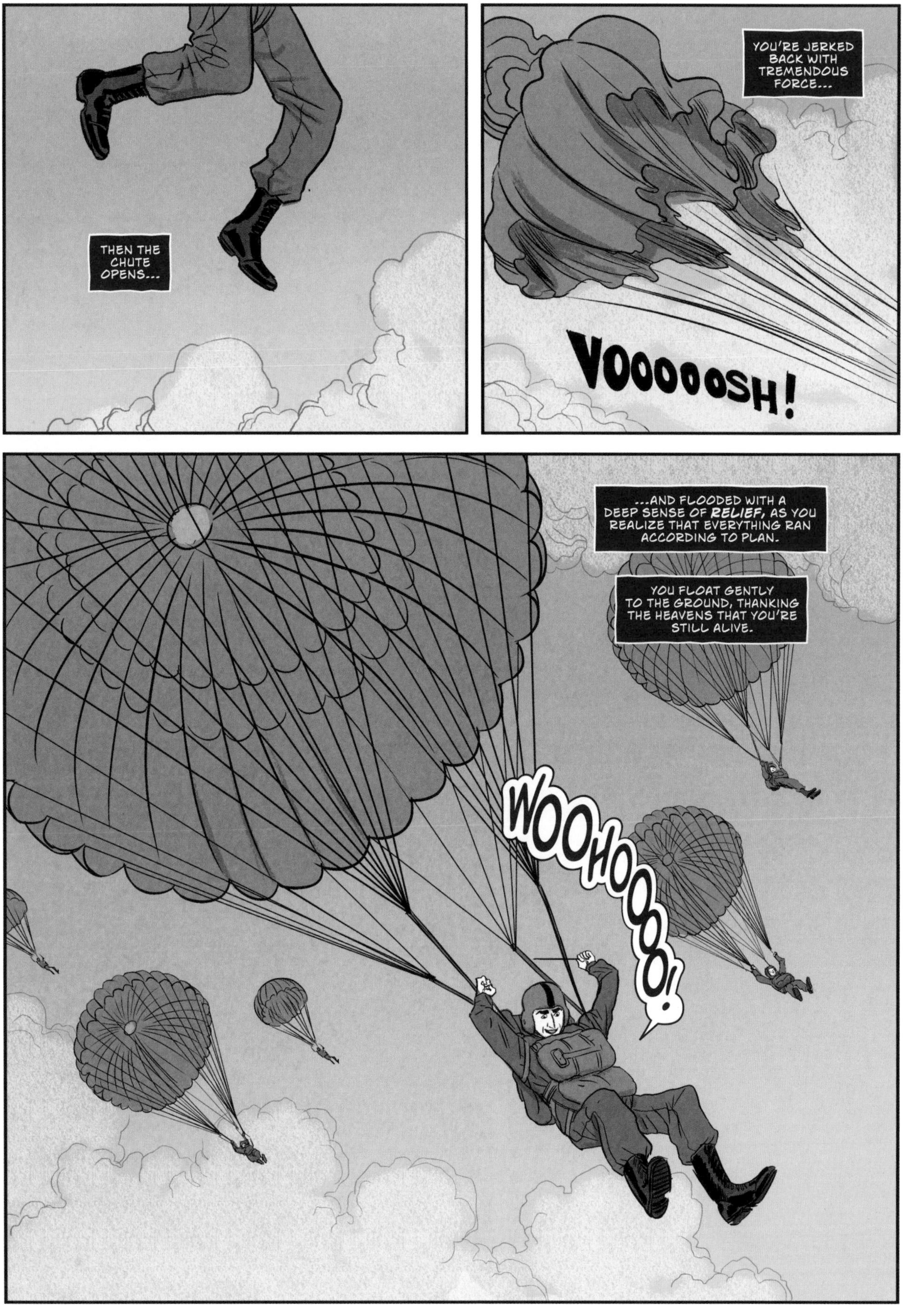
THEN THE CHUTE OPENS...
YOU'RE JERKED BACK WITH TREMENDOUS FORCE...
VOOOOOSH!
...AND FLOODED WITH A DEEP SENSE OF RELIEF, AS YOU REALIZE THAT EVERYTHING RAN ACCORDING TO PLAN.
YOU FLOAT GENTLY TO THE GROUND, THANKING THE HEAVENS THAT YOU'RE STILL ALIVE.
WOOHOOOOO!

BY THE END OF JUMP SCHOOL, ONLY A THIRD OF US--THE MOST RESILIENT OF THE BUNCH--MADE IT.

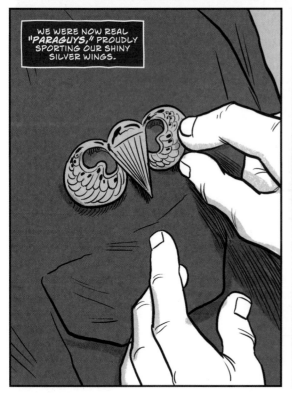

WE WERE NOW REAL *"PARAGUYS,"* PROUDLY SPORTING OUR SHINY SILVER WINGS.

CONGRATULATIONS, SERLING.

OUR NEXT STOP WAS *CAMP POLK*, WHERE WE WERE STATIONED FOR MANEUVERS.

ALL OF A SUDDEN, WE HAD PLENTY OF TIME TO KILL.

YEAHH!

FROM THE RIGHT! *FROM THE RIGHT!*

WOOOO!

I WAS READING TOO MUCH ERNEST HEMINGWAY AND JACK LONDON.

HIGH ON THEIR ROMANTIC IDEAS OF MACHISMO, I DECIDED TO TRY MY HAND AT *BOXING.*

I WAS EAGER TO PROVE TO EVERYONE THAT, IN SPITE OF MY SIZE, I WAS ONE TOUGH TROOPER.

I WAS ON A *ROLL*. I HAD WON SEVENTEEN CONSECUTIVE FIGHTS WHILE REPRESENTING MY REGIMENT.

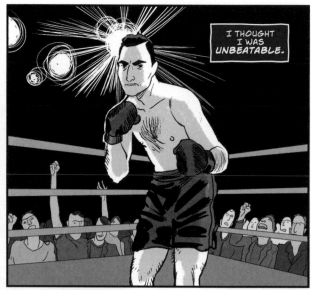

I THOUGHT I WAS *UNBEATABLE*.

WHAM!

MY NOSE WAS BROKEN IN TWO PLACES, AND MY EYE NEARLY *KNOCKED* OUT OF MY HEAD.

I WAS ORDERED TO STOP BOXING.

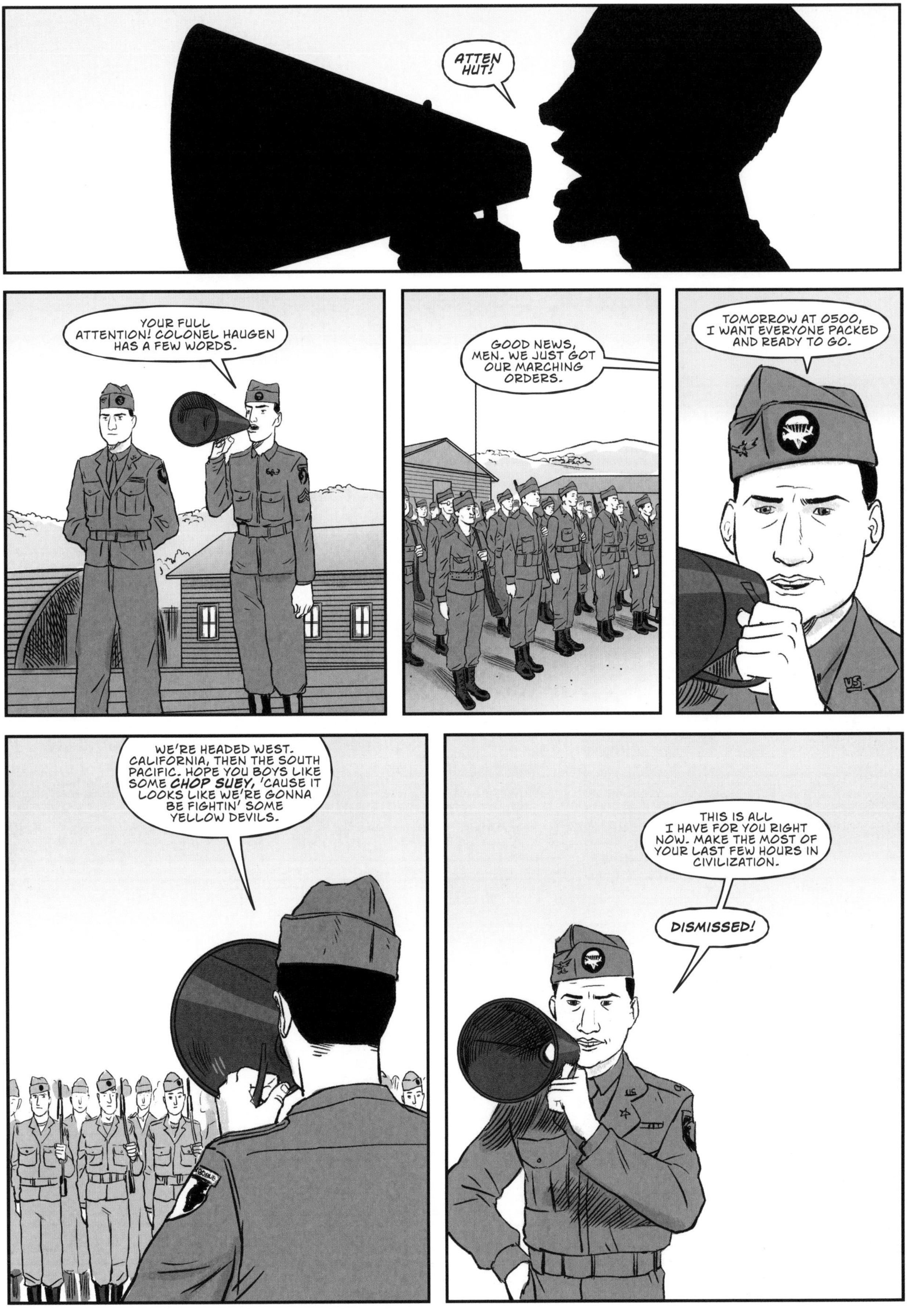
ATTEN HUT!
YOUR FULL ATTENTION! COLONEL HAUGEN HAS A FEW WORDS.
GOOD NEWS, MEN. WE JUST GOT OUR MARCHING ORDERS.
TOMORROW AT 0500, I WANT EVERYONE PACKED AND READY TO GO.
WE'RE HEADED WEST. CALIFORNIA, THEN THE SOUTH PACIFIC. HOPE YOU BOYS LIKE SOME CHOP SUEY, 'CAUSE IT LOOKS LIKE WE'RE GONNA BE FIGHTIN' SOME YELLOW DEVILS.
THIS IS ALL I HAVE FOR YOU RIGHT NOW. MAKE THE MOST OF YOUR LAST FEW HOURS IN CIVILIZATION.
DISMISSED!

WHY THE SOUR FACE, SERLING?

I THOUGHT WE WERE GOING TO FIGHT *GERRY**.

NOW THEY'RE SHIPPING US TO THE *SOUTH PACIFIC?*

MHM-- WHY DON'CHA GO 'N HAVE A CHAT WITH YOUR *BUDDY*, IKE?

I JUST WANNA BE WHERE THE *ACTION* IS!

YOU THOUGHT YOU'D PUMMEL GORING FULL OF LEAD THEN USE THE FÜHRER'S *SKULL* FOR LIBATIONS?

A MAN CAN *DREAM*, CAN'T HE?

DREAM ON!

* SLANG FOR GERMANS

24

THE COMMANDERS KEPT US IN THE DARK AS WE SAILED UP THE PACIFIC.

WE WERE ITCHING FOR BATTLE, BUT WE WOULDN'T SEE IT FOR A *WHILE*.

SOMEHOW, THE JAPANESE FOUND OUT WE WERE COMING.

511TH PARACHUTE INFANTRY ON THE U.S.S. SEA PIKE--WE WELCOME YOU TO THE PACIFIC THEATER.

WE KNOW YOU ARE ON YOUR WAY TO ORO BAY, NEW GUINEA.

REST ASSURED: YOU *WILL* BE *ATTACKED* BY SUBMARINES ON YOUR JOURNEY.

LATER.

COMICS? I THOUGHT YOU WERE AN *INTELLECTUAL*.

DON'T BE A SNOB, THERE'S SOME GOOD STUFF IN HERE.

EVEN A *MARTIAN* COULD DO SHAKESPEARE IF YOU'D ONLY GIVE HIM HALF A CHANCE.

DESPITE THE OMINOUS THREAT AND CHOPPY WATERS, WE KEPT OUR SPIRITS UP.

WE CELEBRATED THE NIGHT WE PASSED THE EQUATOR.

GOOTEN TAG MENCHEN! YOUR PAL, ZE FYUROR, HERE.

ICH VANTED TO TELL YOU: ZER IZ EE BIG PROBLEMA VIZ ZEE *AMERICANZ.*

ICH BIN *HATE* ZEE AMERICANZ. *HATE ZEM!*

BUT DEAR *GOTT...ZER VEEMEN!*

HAVE YOU ZEEN ZEE AMERICAN VEEMEN?! VIZ FRÄULEIN *JANE RUSSELL.* OCH GOTT!

I VOULD LIKE HER TO GIFF ME A *PRIVATE* ZIG HEIL, OHHH, VIZ HER TWO HINDENBERGS!

HAHAHAHAHA

We finally arrived in New Guinea, and were assured that we would soon be deployed on a large scale mission.

In the meantime, we were to undergo "JUNGLE TRAINING," which, in reality, meant doing a whole lot of NOTHING.

FIVE MONTHS WOULD PASS WITH NOTHING TO DO.

SOME MEN DIDN'T TAKE TOO WELL TO THE *WAITING.*

BAM!

I DID MY BEST TO KEEP BUSY, TAKING ONE FINAL STAB AT BOXING.

WHICH ENDED *MISERABLY.*

WHEN THAT DIDN'T WORK, I TRIED *POETRY*.

HEY LEVY, LISTEN TO THIS, TELL ME WHAT YOU THINK...

TAKE COURAGE AND DEVILTRY, COCKINESS, GUTS, MIX 'EM UP WITH A GANG OF THE RIGHT GUYS, GIVE 'EM WINGS AND BOOTS. CALL 'EM PARATROOPS. LET 'EM JUMP WITH CHUTES FROM THE SKIES...WE'RE GOOD AND WE KNOW IT, WE HAVE AND WE'LL SHOW IT, THERE'RE PARAGUYS FIGHTING THIS WAR.

HEY, THAT'S SWELL, ROD! YOU OUGHTTA TRY AND GET IT PUBLISHED!

YEAH? I'LL MAIL IT TO MY BROTHER, SEE WHAT HE THINKS.

THE RESPONSE FROM MY BROTHER BOBBY WAS LESS THAN ENTHUSIASTIC. HE TOLD ME TO *DROP IT*, THAT I WASN'T MEANT TO BE A POET.

RADIO WAS ANOTHER GOOD PASTIME. I WAS A GREAT FAN OF *NORMAN CORWIN* AND IT WAS A *THRILL* TO HEAR HIM DOING HIS PART TO AID THE WAR.

THIS IS WAR! THE FOUR MAJOR NETWORKS JOIN AGAIN TO PRESENT THE SIXTH IN THEIR SERIES OF BROADCASTS FOR WARTIME AMERICA.

OUR PROGRAM TONIGHT IS CALLED "YOU'RE ON YOUR OWN" BY NORMAN CORWIN.

NORMAN CORWIN WAS PERHAPS THE *GREATEST* DRAMATIST OF THE GOLDEN AGE OF RADIO.

HE WAS ALSO ONE OF THE FIRST WRITERS TO USE "ENTERTAINMENT" TO GRAPPLE WITH SERIOUS SOCIAL ISSUES.

HE COVERED MANY FIELDS IN HIS PROGRAMS INCLUDING HISTORY, BIOGRAPHY, POETRY AND CURRENT EVENTS. HE ALSO WROTE DRAMATIC PARABLES, AND HAD A SPECIAL AFFINITY FOR WRITING ABOUT THE *STRUGGLES* AND STRIFE OF THE COMMON MAN.

ORDERS FINALLY CAME IN.

SUDDENLY WE FOUND OURSELVES IN THE MIDST OF A SAVAGE JUNGLE ON THE ISLAND OF LEYTE IN THE PHILIPPINES.

THE ISLAND HAD BEEN WON OVER BY OUR TROOPS BEFORE OUR ARRIVAL, BUT POCKETS OF JAPANESE SOLDIERS WERE STILL ENTRENCHED IN CAVES WITHIN THE MOUNTAINS.

WE WERE TASKED WITH CROSSING THE ISLAND THROUGH THE MAHAGNAO MOUNTAINS AND FLUSHING OUT ANY RESISTANCE.

SOUVENIR, SERLING?

HUH?

MY COUSIN FOUGHT IN GUADAL-CANAL, GOT HIMSELF A NICE COLLECTION OF JAP SKULLS.

AT FIRST, OUR ONLY ENEMY WAS THE *ISLAND ITSELF*--WITH ITS HELLISH TERRAIN AND PUNISHING WEATHER.

THERE WAS NO SIGN OF THE JAPANESE. THE ANTICIPATION WAS NERVE-WRACKING.

WHERE THE FUCK *ARE* THOSE BASTARDS?

I WISH I KNEW.

WHAT'S WRONG WITH HIM?

HE'S BURNIN' UP.

MALARIA.

UNPREPARED FOR THE ROUGH JUNGLE TERRAIN, WE MOVED AT A SNAIL'S PACE, SOMETIMES BARELY A MILE A DAY.

IT WASN'T TOO LONG BEFORE WE HAD OUR FIRST ENCOUNTER WITH THE ENEMY.

HEY SERLING, HAVE YOU SEEN SIMMONS?

NAH, WHAT'S GOIN' ON?

WE JUST DID OUR MORNING HEADCOUNT. HE'S M.I.A.

OVER HERE!

THE JAPANESE MANAGED TO TERRORIZE US. THEY WOULD COME AT NIGHT, KILL SILENTLY, AND DISAPPEAR LIKE GHOSTS.

EVEN MORE TERRIFYING WERE THE SAKE-FUELED *SUICIDE ATTACKS.*

AHHHHHHHHH

HOLY MOSES, WHAT THE *HELL* IS THAT?

BANZAI!

IT'S A LANDMINE!

KA-BOOM!

WE EVENTUALLY FOUND OURSELVES TRAPPED AT THE FOOTHILL OF THE MAHAGNAO VOLCANO. THE AREA WAS COMPLETELY *INFESTED* WITH ENEMY SOLDIERS, AND WE WERE *LOST.*

ARE YOU SURE WE DIDN'T MOVE PAST THE RIDGE?

I'M SURE, CAPTAIN! THIS IS THE CAMPGROUND FROM THREE DAYS AGO.

CHRIST!

WE WERE OFFICIALLY OUT OF RATIONS AND WATER.

GRUMBLE

WE WERE STARVING. I NEVER FELT SUCH HUNGER IN MY LIFE.

FINALLY, RELIEF CAME.

VRRRRRRRRR

OK, MEN! LOOKS LIKE THE BISCUIT BOMBERS ARE FINALLY HERE!

ALL RIGHT!

YIPPEE!

MY PAL LEVY GOT A LITTLE *TOO* EXCITED BY THE NEWS.

CHOW CALL! CHOW CALL, BOYS! HAM AND EGGS BY AIRMAIL!

HAM AND EGGS AND FRIED POTATOES, BOYS!

MAKE IT KOSHER, BOYS! MAKE IT *KOSHER*... EVEN IF YOU HAVE TO DROP A *RABBI!*

FOOOM!

TAKE COVER! TAKE COVER!

IT'S RAINING CHOW! IT'S RAINING CHOW!

LEVY! ARE YOU *NUTS?* TAKE COVER!

LEVY'S DEATH WAS PAINFULLY **SENSELESS.**

GOD, FULL OF MERCY, WHO DWELLS IN THE HEIGHTS, PROVIDE A SURE REST UPON THE DIVINE PRESENCE'S WINGS, WITHIN THE RANGE OF THE HOLY, PURE AND GLORIOUS, WHOSE SHINING RESEMBLE THE SKY'S...

AMEN.

AT TIMES, IT SEEMED THE JUNGLE HAD NO END. AS IF WE WERE TRAPPED IN A LIMITLESS *TROPICAL NIGHTMARE.*

ALRIGHT, MEN, TAKE FIVE.

YOU OWE ME ONE, SERLING.

I SHOULD HAVE DIED THAT DAY.

AFTER WHAT SEEMED LIKE EONS, WE FINALLY BROKE THROUGH THE JUNGLE.

AHOY!

GOOD TO SEE YOU, MAJOR.

CAPTAIN.

A JOB WELL DONE.

WE'LL BE TAKING YOU BACK TO BASE.

WE MADE IT. BUT I DIDN'T FEEL RELIEVED.

I FELT *PETRIFIED.*

IT WAS CHRISTMAS DAY.

MY *BIRTHDAY.*

Dear Dad,

Just as you and Mom thought mainly about some future Christmas—my thoughts were along the same line on my birthday. We were still in combat—but you'd be surprised—a guy can do some thinking in a fox hole.

You know, Dad, if you and I have any differences—and little run-ins occasionally—it's not for you to apologize.

All my life, you've given me everything I've wanted.

I never so much as gave it a thought that you might find it tough to keep supplying me with every whim, and the idea of repaying you never entered my head.

Accordingly, my gratefulness was a shallow, momentary thing that couldn't have made you understand that your efforts were really appreciated.

So Dad, when that future Christmas when we're together again rolls around, you can put aside thoughts of making up for the past—it'll be for me to start showing that the years of you slaving away and worrying just for my benefit were not thrown away on a selfish, thoughtless kid.

WE HAD ACCOMPLISHED OUR MISSION. BUT THERE WAS NO REST FOR US. A FEW HOT MEALS, FRESH UNIFORMS...

...AND WE WERE OFF AGAIN, HEADED FOR A COVERT JUMP ONTO TAGAYTAY.

WE WERE TO PROCEED FROM THERE BY GROUND TOWARDS MANILA.

THE JOKES HAD STOPPED, THE SMILES WIPED AWAY.

WE WERE NOW A GROUP OF AUTOMATONS READY TO BLINDLY FOLLOW ORDERS.

READY ONCE MORE TO JUMP TOWARDS OUR DEATHS.

THE FOLLOWING DAY WE ARRIVED AT THE OUTSKIRTS OF MANILA.

THE CITY LAY IN *RUINS*.

JAPANESE *GENERAL YAMASHITA* HAD, BY THAT POINT, ORDERED HIS FORCES TO RETREAT FROM MANILA.

BUT *ADMIRAL IWABUCHI*, HIS SUBORDINATE WHO COMMANDED THE JAPANESE FORCES IN THE CITY, HAD IGNORED THE ORDERS AND FORTIFIED THE CITY, ORDERING HIS MEN TO FIGHT TO THE DEATH.

山下奉文

岩淵三次

MANILA WAS ONE GREAT DEATH TRAP, AND WE WERE MARCHING STRAIGHT INTO ITS *GAPING MAW*.

LATER.

LADIES AND GENTLEMEN, THE ENTIRE STADIUM IS HOLDING ITS BREATH. WILL JOE GORDON MAKE IT?

AND HE HITS THE BALL! IT'S GOING, *IT'S GOING...*

ENOUGH JOKING AROUND, SERLING. LET'S MOVE IN.

BLAM!

THE CITY WAS SATURATED WITH DEATH AND SUFFERING.

I WANTED TO DO SOMETHING ABOUT IT, BUT *COULDN'T*.

SERLING, FRANK, CHECK THAT STRUCTURE FOR HOSTILES.

I FELT USELESS, OVERWHELMED BY A DEEP SENSE OF FUTILITY.

COME ON, THERE'S NOTHING WE CAN DO.

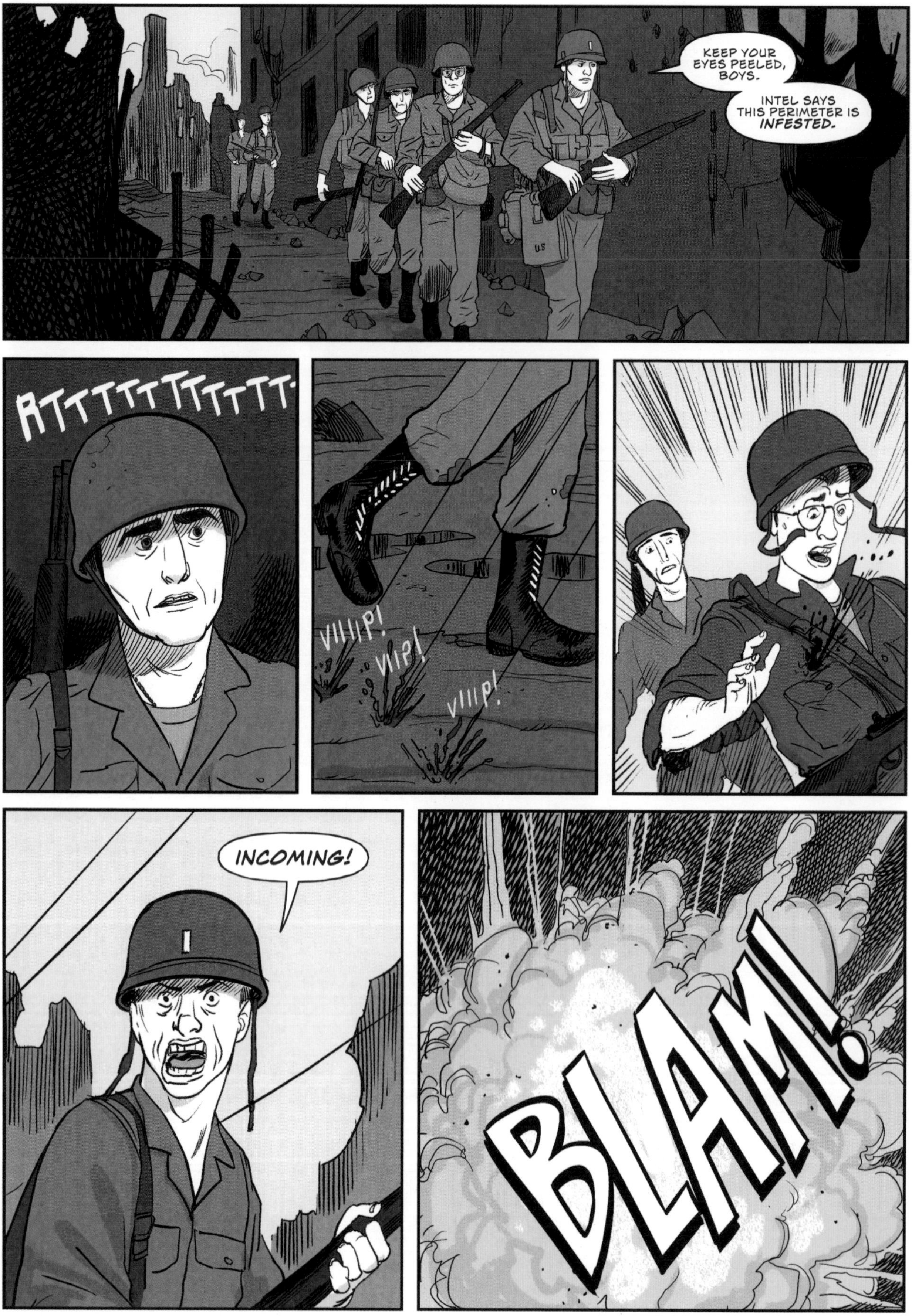
KEEP YOUR EYES PEELED, BOYS.
INTEL SAYS THIS PERIMETER IS INFESTED.
RTTTTTTTTTTTT-
VIIIIP!
VIIP!
VIIIP!
INCOMING!
BLAM!

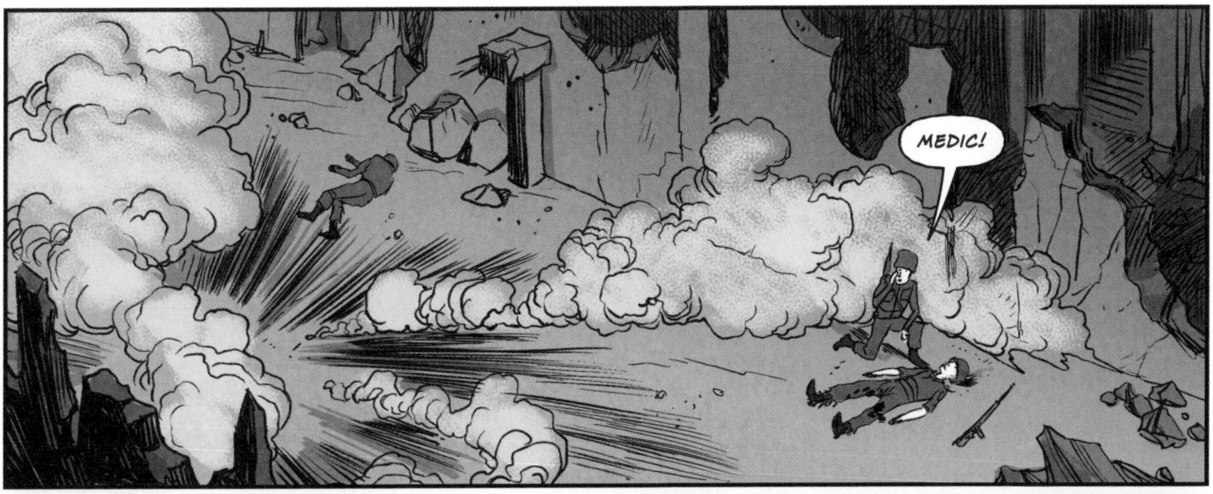
MEDIC!

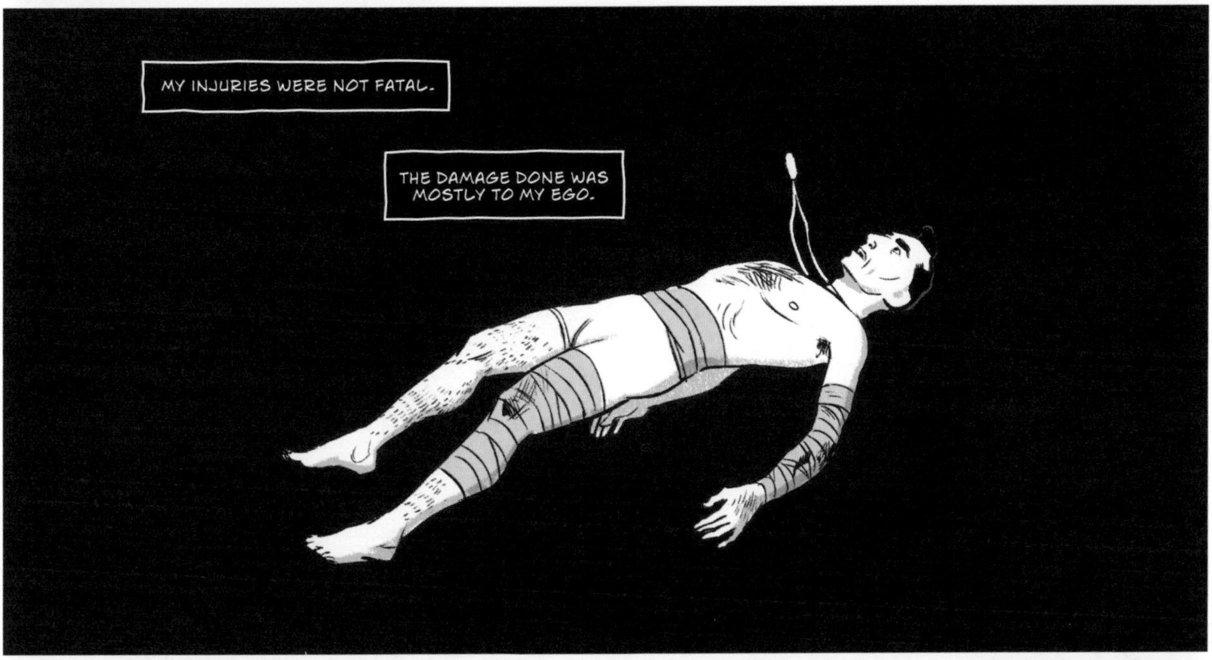
MY INJURIES WERE NOT FATAL.
THE DAMAGE DONE WAS MOSTLY TO MY EGO.

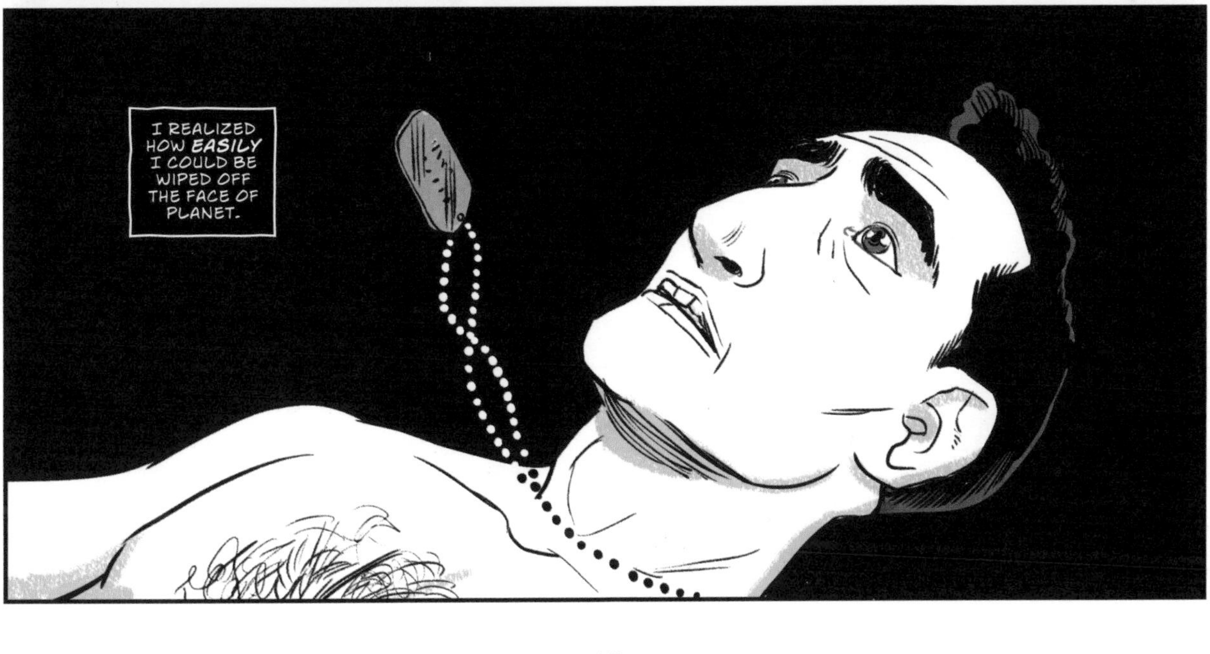
I REALIZED HOW ***EASILY*** I COULD BE WIPED OFF THE FACE OF PLANET.

AFTER A FEW WEEKS IN REHAB, I WAS SENT BACK INTO THE FIELD.

AS I RETURNED TO THE SURREAL REALITY OF BATTLE, IT DAWNED ON ME THAT I WAS NOW PART OF THE *LIVING DEAD*.

STILL BREATHING, STILL MOVING...

WHILE MORE THAN HALF OF MY COMRADES WERE NOW *FOOD* FOR *WORMS*.

THE RANDOMNESS OF IT ALL WAS MIND-BOGGLING.

WHO GOT TO LIVE, AND WHO DIDN'T.

THE FEVER OF WAR WOULD NOT LOOSEN ITS GRIP.

MY ONLY SOLACE WAS THE *PAIN* I SHARED WITH MY FELLOW TROOPS.

THERE WERE RUMORS THAT THE END WAS *NEAR.*

NONE OF US BELIEVED IT.

THEN THEY DROPPED THE BOMB.

AFTER THE JAPANESE SURRENDERED, THE 511TH WAS SHIPPED TO YOKAHAMA, JAPAN, WHERE A TEMPORARY AMERICAN BASE WAS BEING SET UP.

THE PLACE WAS *COMPLETELY* ABANDONED.

IT WAS AS IF EVERYBODY HAD VANISHED OVERNIGHT.

THE CITY WAS RIGGED WITH *EXPLOSIVES*, WHICH MY DIVISION WAS TASKED WITH DISMANTLING.

MAKE SURE TO CUT THEM ALL IN *ONE GO.*

ON IT.

SERGEANT SERLING?

YES?

THERE'S AN URGENT MESSAGE FOR YOU AT THE RED CROSS OFFICES.

SIGN HERE. AND HERE.

THERE YOU GO. APOLOGIES FOR THE DELAY.

THE WAR WAS OVER, BUT IT WAS OVER TOO LATE...

I WOULD NEVER SEE MY FATHER AGAIN.

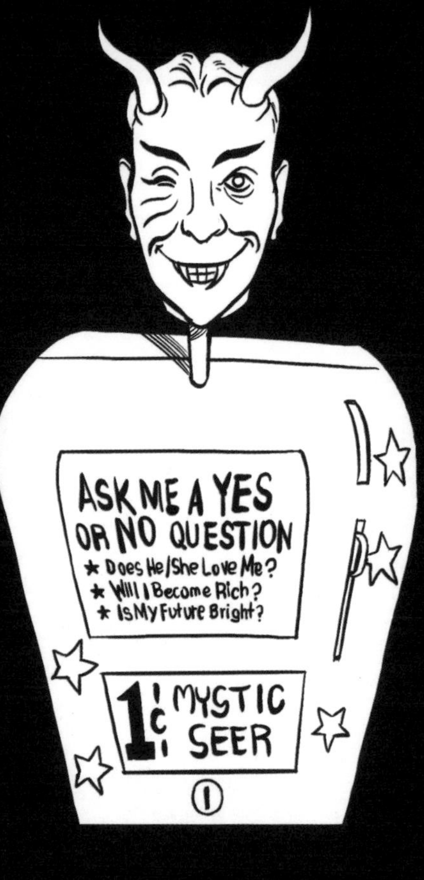
ASK ME A YES OR NO QUESTION
★ Does He/She Love Me?
★ Will I Become Rich?
★ Is My Future Bright?
1¢ MYSTIC SEER

PART II

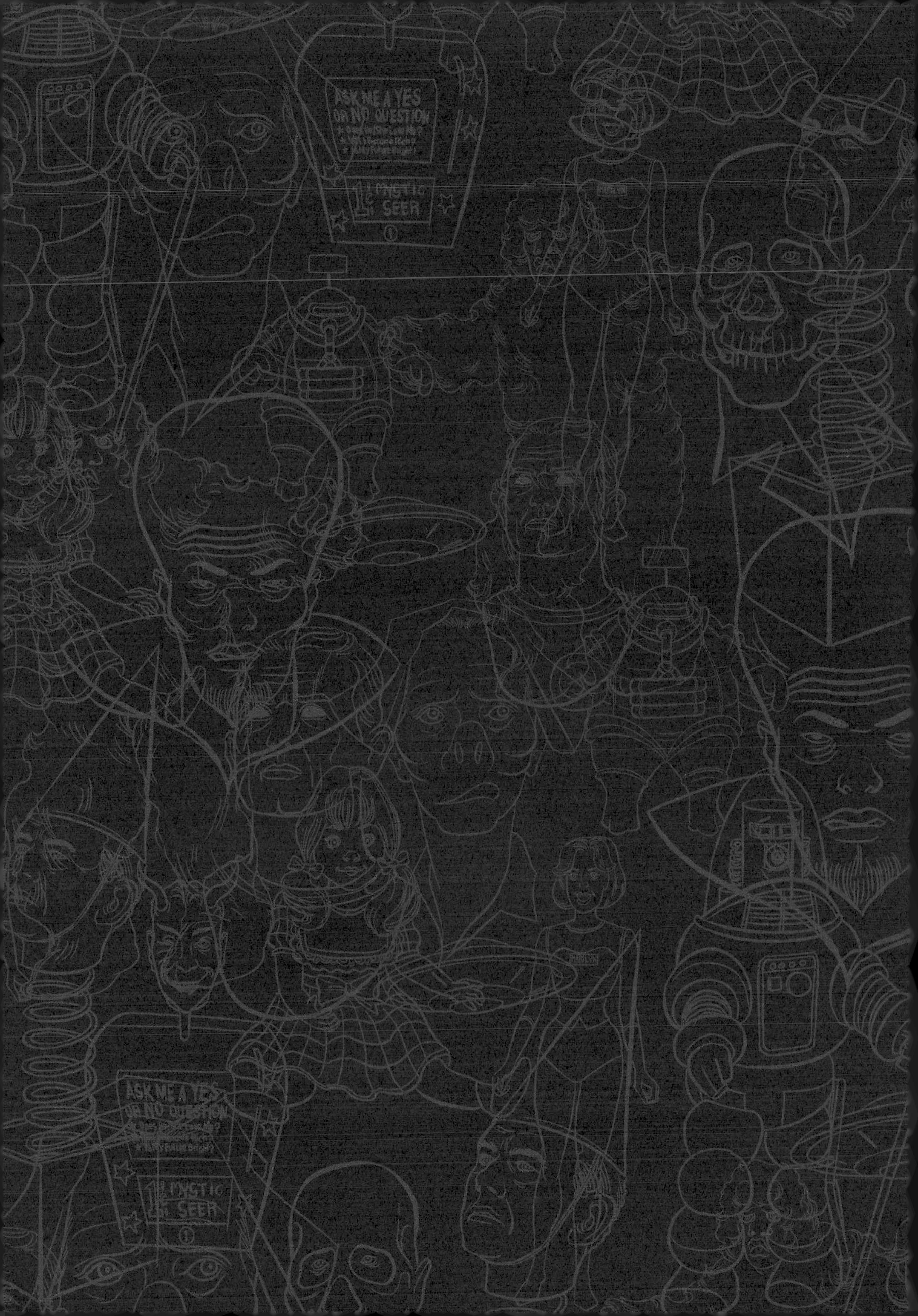
ASK ME A YES OR NO QUESTION
MYSTIC SEER
ASK ME A YES OR NO QUESTION
MYSTIC SEER

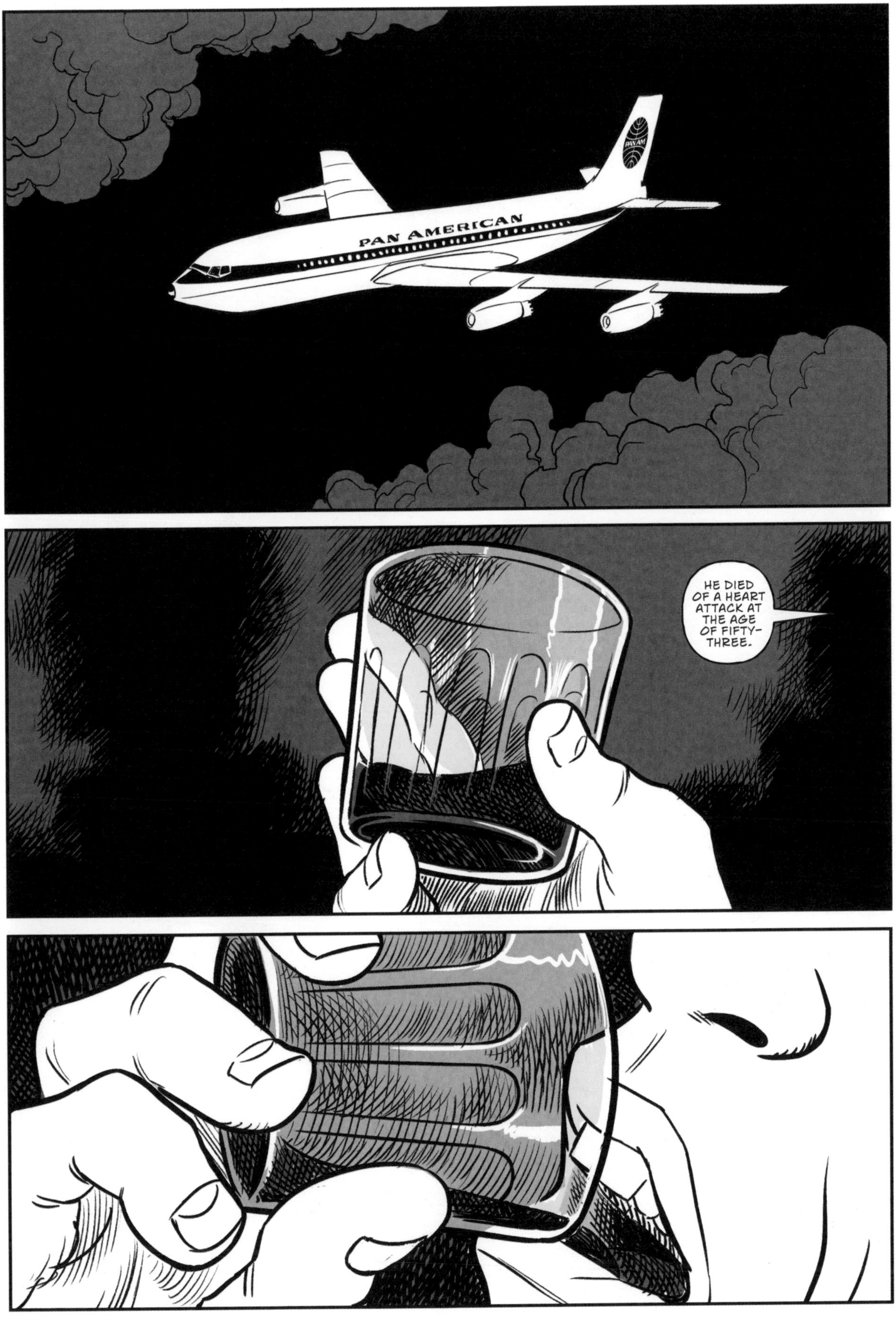
PAN AMERICAN
PAN AM
HE DIED OF A HEART ATTACK AT THE AGE OF FIFTY-THREE.

I'M SORRY TO HEAR THAT.

IT WAS A MISERABLE WAY TO END MY SERVICE. AND DESPITE THE TRAGEDY, THE ARMY WOULDN'T GRANT ME AN EMERGENCY LEAVE.

SOMETHING IN ME **BROKE** THAT DAY... AND I'M NOT SURE IT **EVER** FULLY HEALED.

SO WHAT HAPPENED NEXT? WERE YOU SHIPPED HOME?

YES, EVENTUALLY.

WHEN I GOT BACK HOME, I FOUND MYSELF AT LOOSE ENDS. BITTER ABOUT EVERYTHING AND AT ODDS WITH THE WORLD.

DURING WAR, YOU YEARN FOR THE FAMILIAR. IT'S ALL YOU DREAM ABOUT: THE *FOOD*, THE *FAMILY*, THE *WOMEN*.

BUT ONCE IT'S ALL OVER, AND YOU'RE BACK HOME, YOU REALIZE THERE'S *NOTHING* WAITING FOR YOU. NOTHING BUT A GREAT WIDE *EMPTINESS*.

EACH NIGHT I WOULD BE PLAGUED BY HORRIFIC *NIGHTMARES*.

MEMORIES OF WAR TRANSMUTED INTO DEMONIC MONSTERS.

ABOMINATIONS ARMED TO THE TEETH.

EAGER TO TEAR ME APART.

WHEN I CONSULTED A DOCTOR, HE SAID IT WAS JUST *SHELL SHOCK*, AND WOULD PASS SOON ENOUGH.

CONTRARY TO THE DOCTOR'S PROGNOSIS, NIGHT TERRORS WOULD HAUNT ME FOR THE *REST OF MY LIFE*.

I WAS AT A LOSS FOR WHAT THE *FUTURE* MIGHT HOLD.

WHERE'S ROD?

HE'S IN THE BASEMENT, WORKING ON HIS MODEL PLANES.

STILL? HE'S BEEN DOWN THERE FOR HOURS! DOESN'T HE WANT TO SEE HIS BROTHER? IT'S NOT LIKE I COME UP HERE EVERY OTHER DAY.

MAYBE YOU SHOULD GO AND CHECK ON HIM, BOBBY.

ROD? *CHRIST,* HOW MANY OF THESE HAVE YOU BUILT?

LOOK BOBBY, *NAKAJIMA B5N,* ISN'T SHE A BEAUT?

DRIVING ME CRAZY, THOUGH. CAN'T SEEM TO GET THE COCKPIT COVER TO FIT.

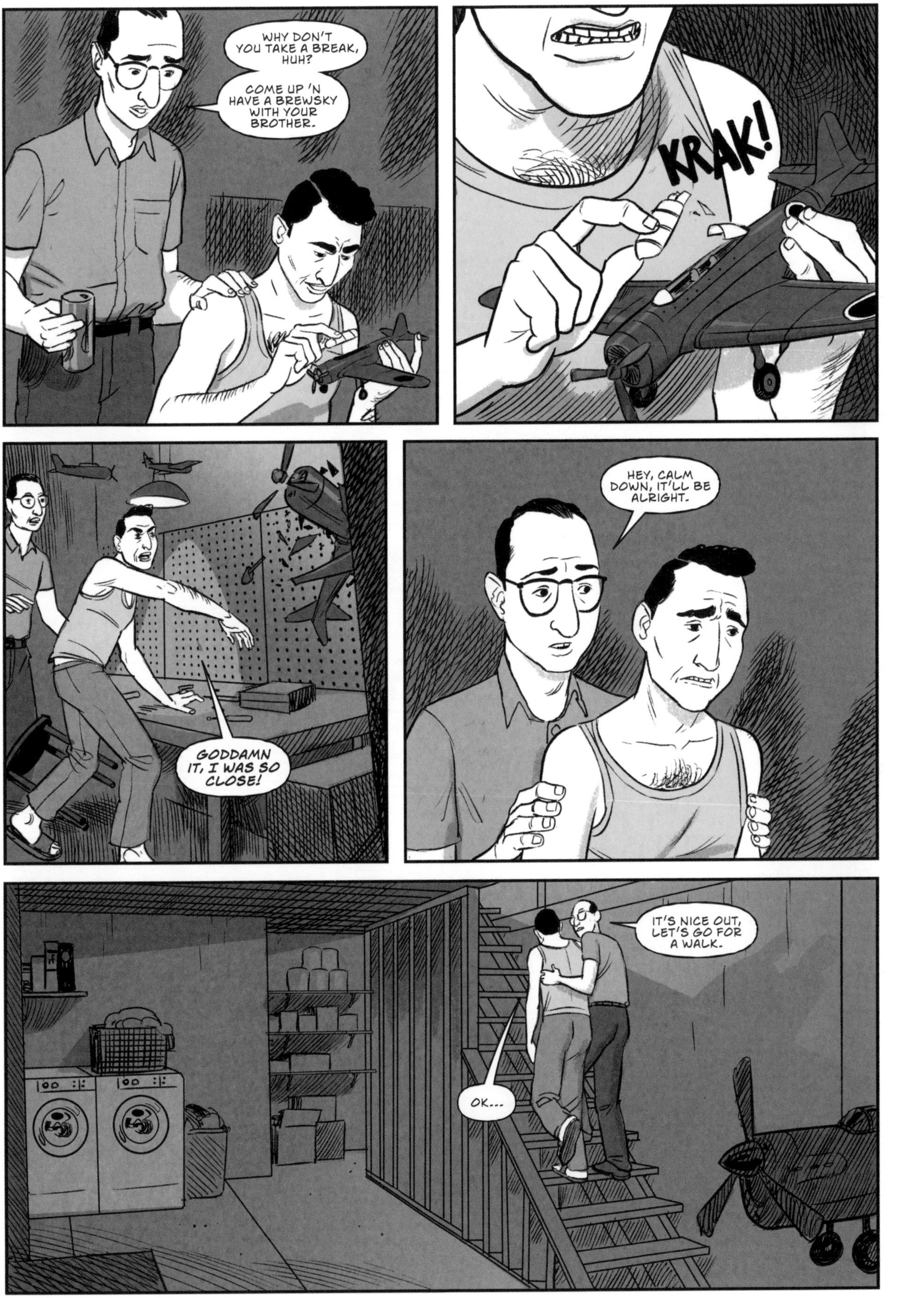
WHY DON'T YOU TAKE A BREAK, HUH?
COME UP 'N HAVE A BREWSKY WITH YOUR BROTHER.
KRAK!
GODDAMN IT, I WAS SO CLOSE!
HEY, CALM DOWN, IT'LL BE ALRIGHT.
IT'S NICE OUT, LET'S GO FOR A WALK.
OK...

EVENTUALLY, I GOT MYSELF TOGETHER. I USED MY G.I. BENEFITS AND ENROLLED AT *ANTIOCH COLLEGE*, MY BROTHER'S ALMA MATER.

ARRIVING IN ANTIOCH WAS A SHOCK TO MY SYSTEM.

AFTER FOUR YEARS OF FIGHTING IN THE RAVENOUS *JUNGLES* AND THE *RUINS* OF MANILA...

...HERE I WAS, CAREFREE, IN A LUSH, SPRAWLING CAMPUS IN YELLOW SPRINGS, OHIO.

AND THE WOMEN!

I FELT LIKE I HAD ARRIVED IN *XANADU*.

I BEGAN TAKING LITERATURE CLASSES, AND SOON FOUND THAT WRITING HELPED ME WORK THROUGH THE PAINFUL MEMORIES OF WAR.

...MAKING A MASTERFUL USE OF THE IRONIC TWIST, O. HENRY PUNISHES HIS PROTAGONIST, SOAPY, JUST AS HE REALIZES IT'S TIME TO CLEAN UP HIS ACT.

PROFESSOR MILLER, I WAS WONDERING IF YOU WOULD GIVE THIS PIECE A READ.

OF COURSE, ROD. SIT DOWN, I'LL READ IT RIGHT NOW.

I THINK YOU REALLY CAPTURED SOMETHING HERE. THERE'S *HEART* IN THIS STORY!

YOU DON'T THINK IT'S TOO DERIVATIVE?

NOT AT ALL. IT'S *HONEST.*

ALL I SEEM TO BE WRITING ARE EITHER WAR STORIES OR BOXING TALES. DON'T YOU THINK THAT'S A PROBLEM?

TWAIN SAID: *"WRITE WHAT YOU KNOW."* YOU KNOW?

YOUR STORY'S FANTASTIC, I THINK WE SHOULD GET THIS PRINTED IN THE ANTIOCHAN. THE PEOPLE NEED TO READ *"THE GOOD RIGHT HAND."*

LIFE WAS FINALLY GETTING BACK ON TRACK. I WAS HAVING A BLAST, GOING OUT WITH ALL THE ANTIOCH LOVELIES.

THE DEPRESSION AND ANXIETY ABATED, OR AT LEAST THAT'S WHAT I *THOUGHT*.

SO, SHIRLEY, WHAT KIND OF VOODOO DID ROD PERFORM TO LAND A DATE WITH YOU, HUH?

AW COME ON, GIVE YOUR LITTLE BROTHER SOME CREDIT.

BOBBY, SOME GALS JUST LIKE MEN WITH MEDALS.

MAYBE THAT'S SOMETHING YOU SHOULDA THOUGHT ABOUT BEFORE YOU AGREED TO SERVE AS A *GLORIFIED PENCIL-PUSHER*.

HIC!

OUCH!

LATER.

AHH...

THIS IS NICE! SPENDING AN EVENING WITH MY BROTHER AND A BEAUTIFUL GAL LIKE YOU...

HIC!

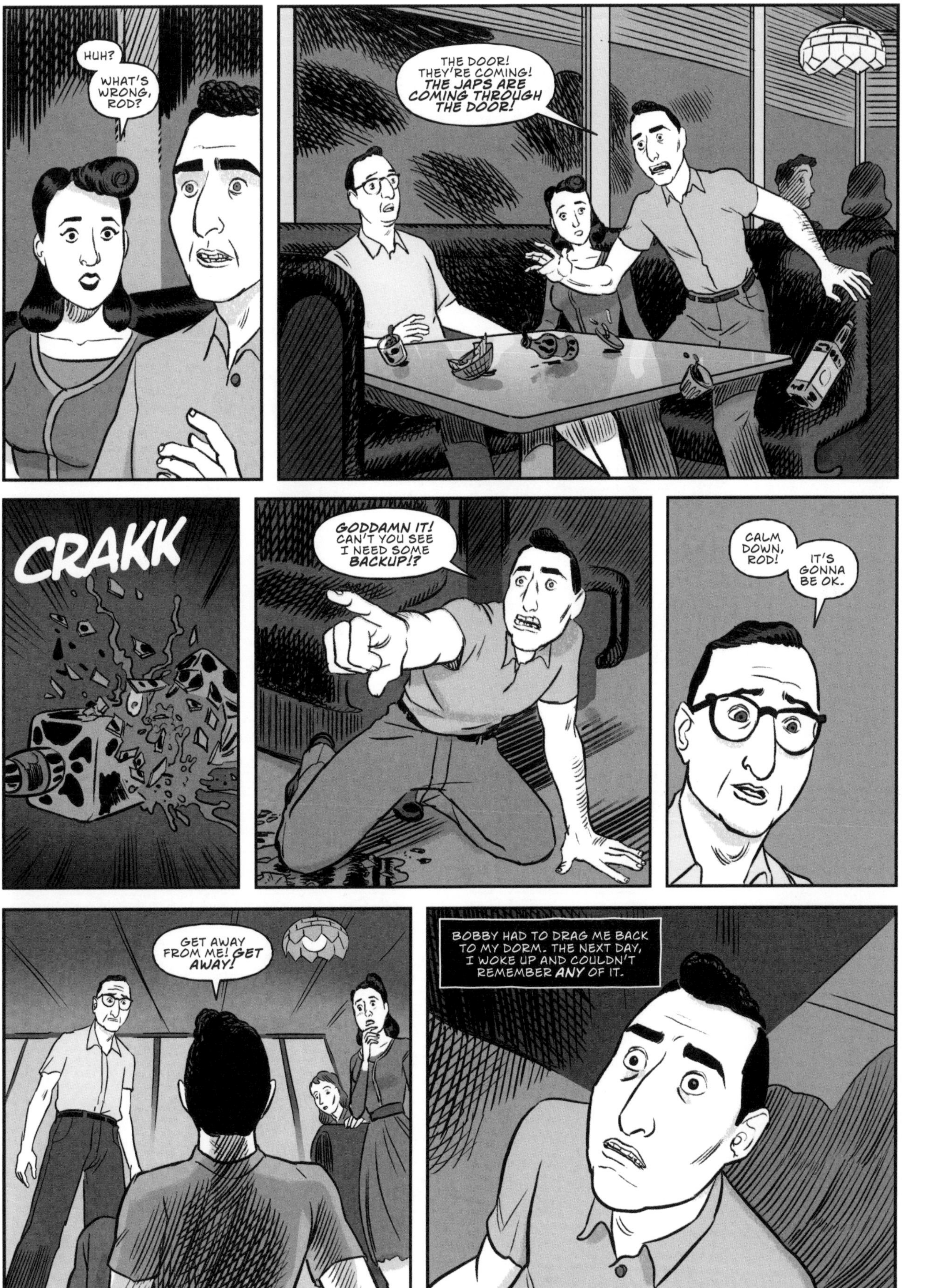

HUH?
WHAT'S WRONG, ROD?
THE DOOR! THEY'RE COMING! **THE JAPS ARE COMING THROUGH THE DOOR!**
CRAKK
GODDAMN IT! CAN'T YOU SEE I NEED SOME **BACKUP!?**
CALM DOWN, ROD!
IT'S GONNA BE OK.
GET AWAY FROM ME! **GET AWAY!**
BOBBY HAD TO DRAG ME BACK TO MY DORM. THE NEXT DAY, I WOKE UP AND COULDN'T REMEMBER **ANY** OF IT.

ANTIOCH HAD A SPECIAL WORK/STUDY PROGRAM. STUDENTS WERE ENCOURAGED TO SPLIT THEIR TIME BETWEEN CAMPUS AND *REAL WORLD EXPERIENCE.*

I WAS ACCEPTED INTO AN INTERNSHIP AT *WNYC* IN NEW YORK CITY.

I WAS EXHILARATED. MANHATTAN WAS THE UNDISPUTED *MECCA* OF RADIO.

BUT I SOON REALIZED THAT THE INTERNSHIP BARELY COVERED MY LIVING EXPENSES.

I HAD TO FIND A WAY TO MAKE ENDS MEET.

NEEDED

FORMER PARATROOPERS FOR EQUIP. EXPERIMENT

HIGHLY LUCRATIVE!

212.592.4431

SO I BEGAN TO TEST *EXPERIMENTAL CHUTES.* I GOT FIFTY BUCKS FOR EACH SUCCESSFUL JUMP.

OK, BOY. THIS ONE'S A DOOZY, SO BE CAREFUL WHEN YOU HIT THE GROUND.

I THINK I CAN HANDLE IT!

UHHH!

THE FOLLOWING DAY, I LIMPED BACK INTO WORK.

ROD!

WHAT HAPPENED TO YOU?

OH... EH... JUST A LITTLE SCUFF I GOT DURING MY SIDE GIG. NO BIG DEAL. WHAT'S ON THE AGENDA FOR TODAY?

ROUGH WEEKEND, HUH?

IN '48, I BECAME THE MANAGER OF THE SCHOOL RADIO STATION, ABS.

IT WAS A DREAM COME TRUE.

AND THAT WAS THE GREAT BING CROSBY, WITH "NOW IS THE HOUR."

BE SURE TO TUNE IN TODAY AT 6 PM, FOR OUR FIRST DRAMATIC RADIO PLAY: "THE FOREVER WAR."

AND THIS IS THE RECORD COLLECTION, WE'RE REORGINIZING.

NEAT.

HEY, ROD, WHO'S THIS?

I'M CAROL, PLEASED TO MEET YOU.

CHARMED.

LET ME SHOW YOU THE RECORDING ROOM.

THERE HE GOES AGAIN.

MAKIN' THE ROUNDS WITH HIS CURRENT SQUEEZE.

POOR GAL, IF ONLY SHE KNEW HOW MANY OTHERS HAVE TAKEN THE TOUR.

CAROL WASN'T JUST ANOTHER SQUEEZE. WE FELL FOR EACH OTHER, HARD. I DECIDED IT WAS TIME TO PROPOSE.

WE ENCOUNTERED RESISTANCE FROM CAROL'S DAD.

WHY **ON EARTH** WOULD YOU WANT TO MARRY A **JEW?** AND HE'S NOT EVEN **WEALTHY!**

AND FROM **MY MOTHER.**

A **SHIKSA,** ROD?

WHAT HAVE I DONE TO DESERVE THIS?

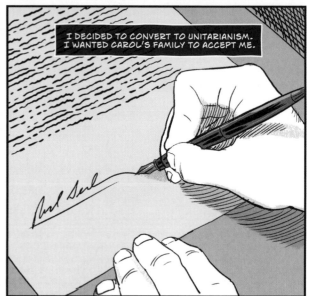

I DECIDED TO CONVERT TO UNITARIANISM. I WANTED CAROL'S FAMILY TO ACCEPT ME.

WE GOT MARRIED THAT SUMMER.

WE MOVED INTO A SURPLUS TRAILER ON CAMPUS. IT WASN'T MUCH, BUT WE WERE TREMENDOUSLY HAPPY TO BE LIVING TOGETHER.

MEANWHILE, I KEPT EXPERIMENTING AT THE SCHOOL STATION.

INSPIRED BY THE WORKS OF NORMAN CORWIN AND ORSON WELLES, I DECIDED TO HELM MY OWN ANTHOLOGY SHOW.

IT WAS, FOR THE MOST PART, A ONE-MAN OPERATION: I WROTE, DIRECTED AND ACTED IN *MANY* OF THE INSTALLMENTS.

YES, I BET THE KEEPER OF THE NORTH STAR THAT THE LITTLE EARTH WOULD DESTROY ITSELF BEFORE THE NEXT BILLION YEARS HAD GONE BY...AND SHE *HAS.*

SHE SEEMS TO HAVE JUST BLOWN HERSELF UP... DISINTEGRATED... SHE NO LONGER EXISTS. *TCH, TCH,* PITY--SHE WAS A LOVELY LITTLE PLANET. WONDER WHAT CAUSED IT?

THAT IS A QUESTION...

OH, WHAT AM I THINKING... I *KNOW* WHAT DESTROYED IT. IT HAD HUMAN BEINGS ON IT.✳

✳FROM "THE BUTTON PUSHERS"

RUNNING A STATION AND PRODUCING MY OWN SHOW ALL WHILE FULLY MATRICULATED TURNED OUT TO BE A *TALL* ORDER.

LUCKY FOR ME, CAROL WAS MORE THAN SUPPORTIVE.

I COULD BOUNCE MY IDEAS OFF HER, AND TRUST HER INSTINCTS.

SHE ALSO CORRECTED MY HORRENDOUS GRAMMAR AND SPELLING.

ROD, THAT'S NOT HOW YOU SPELL "BEGUILED."

I'LL GET IT RIGHT ONE DAY.

YOU KNOW, THIS IS PROBABLY YOUR *BEST* SCRIPT YET.

YOU THINK SO?

I DO. WHY DON'T YOU SUBMIT THIS TO A COMPETITION? MAYBE *THE DR. CHRISTIAN SHOW*?

REALLY? I...I DON'T STAND A CHANCE!

I SUBMITTED THE PLAY AND WON THIRD PRIZE, 500 BUCKS AND AN ALL-EXPENSES-PAID TRIP TO NYC.

LIVE ON THE RADIO, I WOULD TASTE MY FIRST MORSEL OF SUCCESS.

HELLO, ROD, AND **CONGRATULATIONS.** I READ YOUR WINNING SCRIPT, "TO LIVE A DREAM," AND I THOUGHT IT WAS A **FINE** JOB OF WRITING.

THANK YOU, MR. HERSHOLT. YOU'VE NO IDEA HOW THRILLED I AM TO KNOW THAT YOU AND THE JUDGES SELECTED MY SCRIPT AS ONE OF THE WINNERS.

NOW, WHERE DID YOU GET THE IDEA FOR THIS **FINE** STORY YOU WROTE?

WELL, I'VE ALWAYS BEEN FOND OF BOXING. TRIED MY HAND IN THE GOLDEN GLOVES--SINCE YOU'VE READ MY STORY, YOU KNOW WHERE IT ALL TIES IN.

INDEED I DO. AND DO YOU INTEND TO FOLLOW WRITING AS A **PROFESSION?**

I'D LIKE TO, MR. HERSHOLT. IN FACT, THE AMBITION OF MY WIFE AND I--

--AND IS YOUR WIFE SITTING OUT FRONT?

YES, SIR...RIGHT THERE.

WELL, WELL, YOU EX-G.I.S **CERTAINLY** SPECIALIZE IN BEAUTIFUL BRIDES. AND NOW, BACK TO THAT AMBITION OF YOURS.

WELL, WE WANT TO LIVE IN A LARGE HOUSE, IN THE SUBURB OF A LARGE CITY, RAISE A FAMILY, A LOT OF DOGS...AND **WRITE!**

MEANWHILE I KEPT MY GIG AS A GUINEA PIG FOR EXPERIMENTAL AVIATION DEVICES. THE JUMPS WERE GETTING MORE LUCRATIVE, BUT ALSO MORE PERILOUS.

THIS IS IT, DON. ROD'S A GONER, HE WENT TOO FAR THIS TIME.

I MEAN, WHO GETS PAID A THOUSAND BUCKS FOR A *SINGLE* JUMP?

I DUNNO.

WE'VE BEEN HERE FOR HOURS! HE WAS SUPPOSED TO GET HERE AT *TWO*! COME ON, LET'S HEAD BACK.

LET'S JUST CHECK THIS LAST TRAIN.

DON! FRANK! YOU MADE IT!

WHAT THE *HELL* HAPPENED TO YOU?

I WAS TESTING A NEW AIR FORCE EJECTION SEAT. YOU SHOULD HAVE SEEN ME SHOOT UP IN THAT THING! IT WAS LIKE A CIRCUS ACT!

TURNS OUT THE THREE OTHER GUYS WHO TESTED IT WERE *KILLED* BY THE DAMN THING.

BUT HEY, *I* MADE IT!

IN 1950 I GOT OFFERED A JOB AS STAFF WRITER ON WLW CINCINNATI, FOR THE *PRINCELY* SUM OF $70 A WEEK.

I WAS THRILLED! AFTER ALL, THIS WAS ALSO WHERE NORMAN CORWIN HAD GOTTEN HIS START.

I STARTED WRITING SCRIPTS FOR THE STATION. AMBITIOUS AND OVERLY ZEALOUS, I'D HOPED TO AWE THEM WITH MY WRITING TALENT.

CLICK CLICK CLICK

BANG

VoOOsSHH!!

OH BOY, I CAN'T GET ENOUGH OF THESE SPECIAL EFFECTS GUYS! THEY'RE MAGICIANS, I TELL YOU! *MAGICIANS!*

ON AIR

SERLING! I READ YOUR SCRIPT. ARE YOU OFF YOUR ROCKER? AN ORCHESTRA? A NARRATOR? YOU'RE IN CINCINNATI, BOY, NOT *BROADWAY.*

WE WANT SOMETHING THAT WILL CONNECT TO OUR LISTENERS. SOMETHING CLOSER TO THE SOIL!

I UNDERSTAND SIR, I'LL GET YOU A NEW SCRIPT BY TOMORROW MORNING.

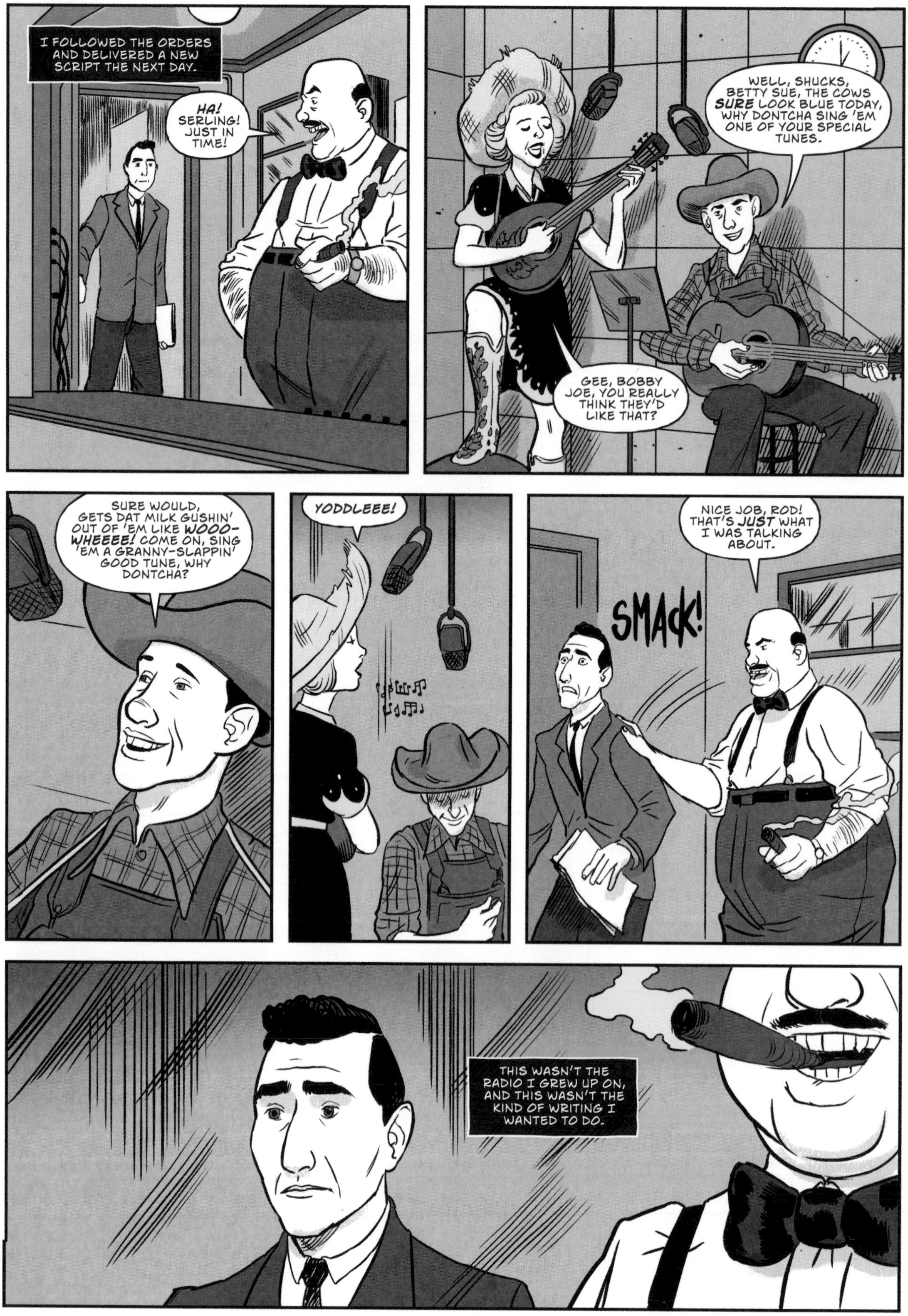
I FOLLOWED THE ORDERS AND DELIVERED A NEW SCRIPT THE NEXT DAY.
HA! SERLING! JUST IN TIME!
WELL, SHUCKS, BETTY SUE, THE COWS SURE LOOK BLUE TODAY, WHY DONTCHA SING 'EM ONE OF YOUR SPECIAL TUNES.
GEE, BOBBY JOE, YOU REALLY THINK THEY'D LIKE THAT?
SURE WOULD, GETS DAT MILK GUSHIN' OUT OF 'EM LIKE WOOO-WHEEEE! COME ON, SING 'EM A GRANNY-SLAPPIN' GOOD TUNE, WHY DONTCHA?
YODDLEEE!
NICE JOB, ROD! THAT'S JUST WHAT I WAS TALKING ABOUT.
SMACK!
THIS WASN'T THE RADIO I GREW UP ON, AND THIS WASN'T THE KIND OF WRITING I WANTED TO DO.

I WAS LEARNING DISCIPLINE, TIME MANAGEMENT AND TECHNIQUE, BUT ALL IN ALL, IT WAS A MURDEROUS GRIND—AND I WAS GROWING DESPERATE TO **BREAK AWAY.**

HI, HONEY.

EVERY DAY I LOOK BACK AT EVERYTHING I WRITE, AND IT'S JUST A BIG HEAP OF **GARBAGE.** I DON'T KNOW HOW MUCH LONGER I CAN HACK IT.

I HAVE FAITH IN YOU. YOU'LL FIGURE THIS OUT.

AFTER COMING HOME FROM A FULL DAY AT THE STATION, I WOULD SIT AND TYPE TV SPEC SCRIPTS INTO THE NIGHT.

THE SCRIPTS WERE ROUGH. THERE'S ONLY SO MUCH LEFT IN YOU AFTER A LONG DAY OF WORK.

OH, ROD. COME TO BED, HONEY. IT'S 2 AM.

AFTER A YEAR OF THIS GRUELING ROUTINE, I MANAGED TO ACCUMULATE OVER FORTY REJECTION SLIPS.

THINGS WERE STARTING TO LOOK *HOPELESS.*

ROD! ROD!

YOU *HAVE* TO SEE THIS!

"DEAR MR. SERLING, IT IS WITH GREAT PLEASURE THAT I INFORM YOU OF OUR DESIRE TO PURCHASE THE RIGHTS TO YOUR SCRIPT TITLED 'GRADY EVERETT FOR THE PEOPLE' FOR THE SERIES STARS OVER BROADWAY!"

THIS IS INCREDIBLE!

"WE ARE OFFERING THE SUM OF $100 FOR BROADCAST RIGHTS. PLEASE RESPOND PROMPTLY TO--"

HEYA, ROD, WE GOT A **NEW ONE** FOR YA.

IS IT **LAXATIVES** AGAIN?

EVEN **BETTER**, WE NEED YOU TO COME UP WITH IDEAS FOR A SHOW THAT WILL PROMOTE A NEW **MIRACLE** MEDICINE.

GERITOL!

THIS THING CAN CURE MORE AILMENTS THAN JESUS CHRIST **HIMSELF!** FROM WHOOPING COUGH TO ULCERS, YOU NAME IT—**GERITOL CURES IT!**

COME ON, BARNIE, NOT ANOTHER ONE...

DON'T ROLL YOUR EYES AT ME, ROD! THIS ONE'S THE **REAL DEAL.** WE NEED YOU TO COME UP WITH A FRESH PITCH, SOMETHING RELATABLE. SOMETHING REAL POPULAR AND CLOSE TO THE SOIL!

THAT AFTERNOON, I HANDED IN MY RESIGNATION.

IN THE EARLY FIFTIES, TELEVISION WAS IN ITS INFANCY--A MEDIUM SEARCHING FOR DIRECTION AND FORM.

AT FIRST, TELEVISION TOOK CUES FROM ITS OLDER SISTER, RADIO, BORROWING A VARIETY OF FORMATS, INCLUDING THE ANTHOLOGY SHOW--A POPULAR FORMAT WHICH PRESENTED A DIFFERENT STORY AND CHARACTER IN EACH EPISODE.

THE EARLY ANTHOLOGY SHOWS WERE SHOT AND BROADCAST *LIVE.* DUE TO THE FORMAT'S LIMITATIONS, THESE "TELEPLAYS" WERE OFTEN SET IN VERY FEW LOCATIONS, AND SHOT IN A SINGLE STUDIO.

TELEVISION DRAMATISTS, SUCH AS PADDY CHAYEFSKY AND GORE VIDAL, WERE ABLE TO USE THESE LIMITATIONS TO THEIR ADVANTAGE. THEY CREATED CHARACTER-DRIVEN NARRATIVES AND INTIMATE SETTINGS THAT WERE PERFECT FOR THE SMALL SCREEN.

MA, SOONER OR LATER, THERE COMES A POINT IN A MAN'S LIFE WHEN HE'S GOTTA FACE SOME FACTS. AND ONE FACT I GOTTA FACE IS THAT, WHATEVER IT IS THAT WOMEN LIKE, *I AIN'T GOT IT.*

THE PLAYS WOULD BE REHEARSED AHEAD OF THE SHOOT AND INCLUDED THE COMPLEX ACROBATICS OF CAMERA MOVES.

LIVE

THEATER WAS NOW PROJECTED INTO MILLIONS OF HOMES THROUGH THE MARVEL OF THE *CATHODE TUBE.*

THE WHOLE OPERATION HAD TO RUN LIKE A WELL-OILED CLOCK. THERE WERE NO SECOND TAKES, ONLY ONE CHANCE TO GET IT RIGHT.

TELEPLAYS WERE IMBUED WITH A SPECIAL ENERGY, SINGULAR TO LIVE TELEVISION. THEY WERE CRUDE, BUT HAD RAW ESSENCE THAT EXISTED *NOWHERE ELSE.*

ADS WERE SOMETIMES SHOT LIVE ON THE SAME SET AS THE SHOW. THE OMNIPOTENT SPONSORS PROVIDED THE CAPITAL FOR PRODUCTION.

LIGHT UP A LUCKY! IT'S LUCKY TIME. BE HAPPY GO LUCKY! IT'S LIGHT-UP TIME.

THE ADS WERE AN UNFORTUNATE DISRUPTION-- EJECTING THE VIEWER FROM THE PLAY AND INTO A WORLD OF KLEENEX, STOVE TOPS, AND SOFT DRINKS.

LUCKY STRIKE

'IT'S TOASTED'

FOR THE TASTE YOU LIKE, LIGHT UP A LUCKY STRIKE!

RELAX! IT'S LIGHT-UP TIME.

BUT THIS WAS *THE GOLDEN AGE OF TELEVISION.* IT WAS AN EXCITING TIME OF RELATIVE ARTISTIC FREEDOM AND AMBITIOUS UNDERTAKINGS.

I WAS IN *LUCK.* STANDING AT THE PRECIPICE OF A NEW INDUSTRY THAT WAS IN DIRE NEED OF NEW TALENT.

TELEVISION WOULD GOBBLE ME RIGHT UP! TAKE ITS CHANCE WITH A COMPLETE UNKNOWN.

IT WAS 1951. OVER THE COURSE OF TWO YEARS, I SLOWLY GAINED A STEADY FOOTING IN THE WORLD OF TELEVISION.

I WAS CONTACTED BY LITERARY AGENT BLANCHE GAINES IN NYC WHO OFFERED ME REPRESENTATION.

TAXI!

66TH AND LEX, AND *STEP ON IT!* WE'RE LATE FOR A MEETING.

YES, MA'AM.

FIRST OFF, WHY ARE YOU STILL LIVING IN CINCINNATI? THE *ACTION* IS *RIGHT HERE.*

WE'VE ONLY RECENTLY BOUGHT OUR HOUSE, AND WE'RE STILL PAYING THE MORTGAGE--

YOU'RE THINKING TOO SMALL, ROD. I NEED YOU TO START THINKING *BIGGER!*

WELL, I CAN'T JUST PACK UP AND LEAVE.

NOT YET, AT LEAST.

VERY WELL, I HOPE YOU LIKE AIRPORTS, BECAUSE YOU'LL BE *JETTING* HERE EVERY OTHER WEEK.

IF THAT'S WHAT IT TAKES.

I'LL BE WORKING TO SELL YOUR TELEPLAYS, BUT I'M GOING TO NEED *YOU* TO START SELLING *ROD SERLING.*

I'LL BE YOUR "FOOT IN THE DOOR," BUT *YOU* GOTTA PUSH TOO! FOR STARTERS--GET YOURSELF A GOOD SUIT. THIS MID-WESTERN *SCHMATTA* WON'T CUT IT IN MANHATTAN.

FOUR MORE YEARS WOULD PASS. GAINES DID AS SHE PROMISED AND MY CAREER WAS MOVING FORWARD AT A STEADY PACE.

I WAS STILL LARGELY UNKNOWN, BUT MADE MY WAY INTO WRITING A FEW RESPECTABLE PROGRAMS.

ON A COLD JANUARY NIGHT IN 1955, CAROL AND I WERE OFF VISITING RELATIVES IN UPSTATE NEW YORK. A BABYSITTER WAS WATCHING OUR FIVE-YEAR-OLD DAUGHTER, *JODI*.

THE KRAFT TELEVISION THEATRE COMES TO YOU *LIVE* FROM NEW YORK.

THE PLAY IS PERFORMED AT THE MOMENT YOU SEE IT--LIVING THEATER FOR YOUR BEST ENTERTAINMENT.

KRAFT
Television Theatre

ONE OF MY TELEPLAYS WAS SET TO BE BROADCAST THAT NIGHT. I HAD *NO IDEA* OF THE IMPACT IT WOULD HAVE.

TONIGHT WE PRESENT THE FOUR HUNDRED AND SIXTY-THIRD PLAY IN THIS SERIES:

"PATTERNS" BY ROD SERLING.

PATTERNS

"PATTERNS" TELLS THE STORY OF *FRED STAPLES*, AN IDEALISTIC YOUNG MAN COMING FROM OHIO TO WORK ON WALL STREET AS A JUNIOR EXECUTIVE.

HE BEGINS WORKING UNDER AN OLDER MAN, BUT SOON DISCOVERS HE'S BEING *GROOMED* TO REPLACE HIM BY THE COMPANY'S RUTHLESS OWNER.

ANDY SLOAN WAS YOUR *CONSCIENCE.* HE WAS A CONSTANT, NAGGING REMINDER THAT SOME THINGS ARE *WRONG.*

KEEP GOING, FRIEND.

YOU WANTED HIM *OUT* BUT YOU WOULDN'T FIRE HIM!

YOU USED HIM AS A *WHIPPING BOY,* TO TRY AND MAKE HIM QUIT. YOU MADE HIM BACKTRACK AND KNUCKLE UNDER AND YOU FINALLY *BEAT* HIM TO DEATH.

THAT'S TRUE.

RING RING

SERLING RESIDENCE.

NO, MR. SERLING IS NOT HOME AT THE MOMENT-- YES. I'M WRITING IT DOWN... PRODUCER, CBS ...*MMM HMM*... YES. GOT IT.

RING RING

HELLO? YES IT IS. NO HE'S NOT. YES I CAN TAKE A MESSAGE...

RING RING

GOOD GRIEF!

"PATTERNS" IS A STORY OF POWER, AMBITION AND THE PRICE TAG THAT HANGS ON SUCCESS. IT IS ALSO A CONFLICT OF YOUTH VS. AGE. FOR EVERY MAN THAT MOVES UP, SOMEONE ELSE HAS TO MOVE OUT...

THE SHOW *HIT A NERVE*, AND WAS A BIG CRITICAL AND COMMERCIAL SUCCESS.

AUDIENCES LOVED IT SO MUCH THAT THEY DEMANDED--AND GOT--A SECOND *LIVE* SCREENING. *A FIRST IN THE HISTORY OF TELEVISION.*

"PATTERNS" TURNED ME INTO AN OVERNIGHT SUCCESS. THE OFFERS CAME LIKE A MONSOON.

I RECEIVED TWENTY-THREE OFFERS FOR TELEVISION WRITING ASSIGNMENTS.

FOURTEEN REQUESTS FOR INTERVIEWS IN LEADING MAGAZINES AND PAPERS.

THREE MOTION PICTURE SCREENWRITING ASSIGNMENTS.

TWO OFFERS FROM BROADWAY PRODUCERS.

AND TWO OFFERS TO WRITE NOVELS.

I HAD THE SAME ANSWER TO THEM ALL:

YES!

I SOON REALIZED WHAT A MISTAKE I'D MADE. I BIT OFF MORE THAN I COULD *CHEW.*

I WAS FAILING TO PRODUCE MATERIAL WITH THE SAME LEVEL OF FINESSE AS "PATTERNS."

THERE WERE SUDDENLY BUYERS FOR ALL MY UNPRODUCED SCREENPLAYS.

...I TELL YA, "PATTERNS" JUST KNOCKED ME OFF MY SEAT. ROD, YOU MADE SOMETHING *SPECIAL*-- AND THAT'S RARE IN OUR BUSINESS.

YOU DON'T MIND IF I CALL YOU *ROD*, DO YOU?

NOT AT ALL!

NOW LISTEN, I KNOW WE'VE ALREADY COMMISSIONED SEVERAL SCREENPLAYS FROM YOU, BUT I WAS WONDERING...

IS IT POSSIBLE THAT YOU HAVE SOMETHING LYING AROUND YOUR OFFICE? SOMETHING *UNPRODUCED?*

WELL, YES, I HAVE SEVERAL SCREENPLAYS. AS A MATTER OF FACT, YOU HAVE FORMERLY REJECTED A FEW OF THEM--

REJECTED? THAT'S THE PAST, ROD! THIS IS THE *DAWNING OF A NEW AGE* FOR YOU. FOR US!

MY REJECTS DRAWER WAS CLEANED OUT. THERE MUST HAVE BEEN TWENTY SCRIPTS OF MINE TELECAST THAT SEASON. MANY OF THEM EMBARRASSINGLY MEDIOCRE.

YES, CAN YOU BELIEVE IT, CAROL? THE *VERY SAME* SCRIPTS THEY REJECTED LAST YEAR!

ONE OF THE TELEPLAYS SOLD WAS "THE RACK." IT WAS SET FOR PRODUCTION ON *THE UNITED STATES STEEL HOUR.*

I READ ABOUT KOREAN WAR P.O.W.S WHO WERE TORTURED, BRAIN-WASHED AND FORCED INTO *FALSE* CONFESSIONS BY THE CHINESE.

POWS RETURN, TRAITORS OR HEROES?

WELCOME THE O HOME

STILL HAUNTED BY MEMORIES OF WAR, AND THE GHOSTS OF MY FALLEN FRIENDS-- I WAS IMMEDIATELY STRUCK BY THE POTENTIAL OF THE STORY.

I WROTE OUT A SCRIPT ABOUT A CERTAIN CAPTAIN EDWARD HALL--A P.O.W. COURT-MARTIALED FOR TREASON AFTER BEING *TORTURED* AND FORCED TO SIDE WITH THE ENEMY.

THE MORALITY OF "THE RACK" WAS PAINTED IN SHADES OF GREY. CAPTAIN HALL WAS NEITHER CLEARLY *GUILTY* NOR *INNOCENT.*

THAT DECISION WAS LEFT TO THE *VIEWERS.*

COWARDICE DOES NOT OCCUR WHERE BRAVERY ENDS. IT IS NOT *EITHER OR.*

FOR IF IT WERE, ALL MEN WOULD BE *HEROES* OR *COWARDS.*

I HUMBLY SUBMIT TO THE COURT THAT THERE MUST BE AN IN-BETWEEN.

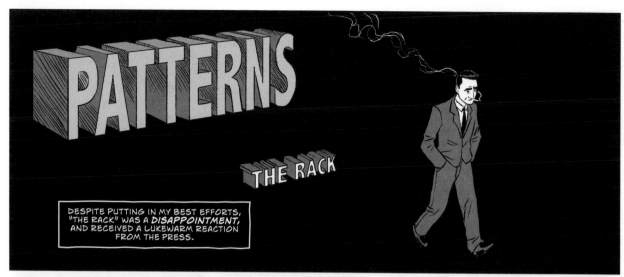

PATTERNS

THE RACK

DESPITE PUTTING IN MY BEST EFFORTS, "THE RACK" WAS A *DISAPPOINTMENT*, AND RECEIVED A LUKEWARM REACTION FROM THE PRESS.

THE FIRST REVIEWS AFTER "PATTERNS" WERE CHARITABLE, AS IF THE THE CRITICS WERE WARY OF THROWING BRICKS AT A SUCCESSFUL AUTHOR.

BUT AFTER TIME, WHEN THE COMPARISONS WITH "PATTERNS" WERE OBVIOUSLY NEGATIVE, THE NEEDLE WAS UNSHEATHED.

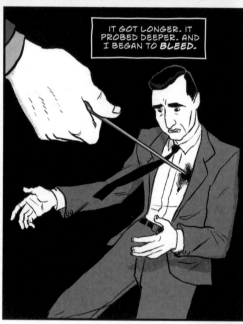

IT GOT LONGER. IT PROBED DEEPER. AND I BEGAN TO *BLEED*.

"GARRITY'S SON"

"THE CHAMPION"

"TO WALK AT MIDNIGHT"

WITH EACH NEW REVIEW, THE BLEEDING GOT WORSE.

AS THE PRESSURE TO DELIVER ANOTHER CRITICAL SUCCESS WAS MOUNTING...

...I BEGAN TO THINK I WOULD *NEVER* CREATE ANYTHING THAT WOULD LIVE UP TO THE QUALITY OF "PATTERNS."

ALL THE WHILE, I WAS STILL INUNDATED WITH THE TOWERING MOUNTAIN OF PROJECTS I'D ACCEPTED.

I DECIDED SOME MAJOR CHANGES WERE DUE.

AFTER SOME DELIBERATION, I DECIDED TO FIRE MY AGENT, BLANCHE GAINES, AND REPLACE HER WITH ASHLEY STEINER, A MAJOR TALENT AGENCY.

IT WAS A DECISION THAT CAME WITH ABOUT TWO TONS OF *SOLID GUILT.*

BLANCHE HAD BEEN THERE FOR ME FROM THE START, BUT AT THIS POINT, SHE WAS UNABLE TO COPE WITH THE SHEER *SCOPE* OF MY PROJECTS.

I ALSO STOPPED TYPING MY SCRIPTS, AND BEGAN USING A DICTAPHONE.

YOU KEEP IT UP, CHUM. JUST KEEP IT UP.

YOU'RE GOING TO TALK YOURSELF INTO A CORNER.

I WAS NOW ABLE TO GENERATE SCRIPTS FASTER THAN EVER.

ONE PROJECT WAS ESPECIALLY CLOSE TO MY HEART. IT WAS A TALE OF SOCIAL CRITIQUE.

REC

A PLAY INSPIRED BY *THE EMMETT TILL CASE.*

WHEN THE STORY FIRST APPEARED, I WAS SHOCKED AND HORRIFIED BY THE WHOLE AFFAIR.

TILL, A FOURTEEN-YEAR-OLD BLACK BOY, WAS VISITING MISSISSIPPI IN THE SUMMER OF '55. AFTER ALLEGEDLY WHISTLING AT CAROLYN BRYANT-- A WHITE WOMAN IN A LOCAL GROCERY STORE--

...TILL WAS KIDNAPPED AND *BRUTALLY MURDERED* BY BRYANT'S HUSBAND AND HIS STEP-BROTHER.

AFTER THE BOY'S BODY EMERGED FROM THE TALLAHATCHIE RIVER, THE TWO WERE PUT ON TRIAL, THEN PROMPTLY ACQUITTED BY AN *ALL WHITE* JURY.

LISTEN, ROD, I KNOW WE'VE TOLD YOU THAT U.S. STEEL ALREADY APPROVED "NOON ON DOOMSDAY."

BUT...THINGS HAVE CHANGED. WE'VE HIT A *SNAG.*

WHAT *KIND* OF SNAG?

WE HAD A PRESS RELEASE STATING THAT YOU WERE WORKING ON A PLAY BASED ON THE EMMETT TILL CASE.

YES. WAS THERE A *PROBLEM?*

YOU COULD SAY SO. WE'VE RECEIVED SEVERAL LETTERS PROTESTING THE SHOW, PREDOMINANTLY FROM A SOUTHERN ORGANIZATION CALLED *THE WHITE CITIZENS COUNCIL**, THEY ARE THREATENING A FULL BOYCOTT OF U.S. STEEL.

WHAT ARE THEY GOING TO DO? BUILD THEIR HOMES OUTTA *TIN FOIL?*

FUNNY! LET ME CUT TO THE CHASE-- WE WOULD LOVE TO PRODUCE THE SHOW, BUT THE SPONSORS ARE NOW DEMANDING SOME MAJOR CHANGES.

CHANGES? *LIKE WHAT?* I'VE ALREADY SHIFTED IT AWAY FROM BLACK VS. WHITE.

*A SOUTHERN WHITE SUPREMACIST ORGANIZATION

WELL, IT'S NOT ENOUGH. I KNOW THAT WE AGREED TO A JEWISH PAWNBROKER AS A GOOD SOLUTION, BUT THE SPONSORS ARE REQUESTING YOU CHANGE THAT AS WELL. NO MINORITIES.

DO THEY KNOW A *KIKE'S* WRITING THIS?

YOU ALSO NEED TO MOVE THE STORY AWAY FROM THE SOUTH. THE SPONSORS SUGGESTED *NEW ENGLAND.*

AND THE VILLAIN NEEDS TO BE SOFTENED. THE SPONSORS ARE ASKING FOR "A GOOD, DECENT AMERICAN BOY, *MOMENTARILY* GONE WRONG."

OH, AND YOU WOULD NEED TO TAKE OUT THE WORD "LYNCH," THEY'RE WORRIED THAT IT SOUNDS *TOO SOUTHERN.*

THERE'S A FULL LIST OF THE REQUESTS ON MY DESK. WE WOULD *PAY* FOR THE CHANGES, OF COURSE.

YOU'RE JUST GOING TO *SIT THERE* AND LET SOME WHITE SUPREMACISTS *JERK* THE NETWORK AROUND LIKE THAT?!

HE *WAS.* I AGREED TO MAKE THE CHANGES, BUT INSIDE I WAS *LIVID.*

MY SCRIPT WAS *EVISCERATED.*

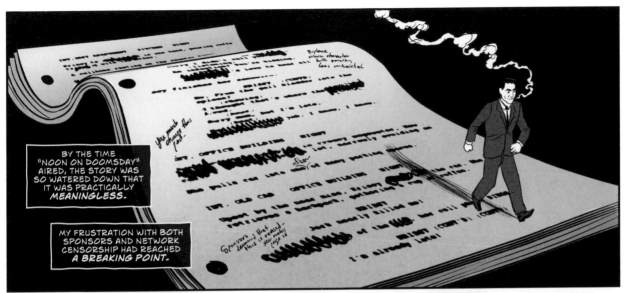

BY THE TIME "NOON ON DOOMSDAY" AIRED, THE STORY WAS SO WATERED DOWN THAT IT WAS PRACTICALLY *MEANINGLESS.*

MY FRUSTRATION WITH BOTH SPONSORS AND NETWORK CENSORSHIP HAD REACHED *A BREAKING POINT.*

I BEGAN TO USE MY NEW STATUS AS A TELEVISION HEAVYWEIGHT TO VOCALIZE MY FRUSTRATIONS.

NO DRAMATIC ART FORM SHOULD BE DICTATED AND CONTROLLED BY MEN WHOSE TRAINING AND INSTINCTS ARE TO *SELL CONSUMER GOODS.*

IT'S DIFFICULT TO PRODUCE A TELEVISION SHOW THAT IS BOTH INCISIVE AND PROBING--

--WHEN EVERY TWELVE MINUTES ONE IS INTERRUPTED BY TWELVE *DANCING RABBITS* SINGING ABOUT *TOILET PAPER.*

TV'S NEWEST ANGRY YOUNG MAN TAKES OFF HIS GLOVES

OVER THE NEXT FEW YEARS I KEPT TAKING SWINGS AT MY **IMMATERIAL OPPONENTS.**

THE ALL-POWERFUL **SPONSORS.**

THE RIGID **NETWORKS.**

THE IRRATIONAL **CENSORS.**

BUT IT WAS **POINTLESS.**

I COULDN'T BEAT THE SYSTEM FROM **WITHIN.**

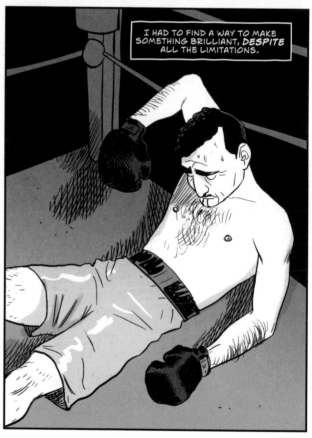

I HAD TO FIND A WAY TO MAKE SOMETHING BRILLIANT, **DESPITE** ALL THE LIMITATIONS.

BY 1956, THE PRESSURE TO PRODUCE ANOTHER HIT HAD BECOME UNBEARABLE.

WE HAD INVITED FRIENDS TO WATCH MY NEWEST TELEDRAMA: "REQUIEM FOR A HEAVYWEIGHT."

I WAS MORE PESSIMISTIC THAN EVER.

SIT DOWN, ROD! YOU'RE MAKING ME *DIZZY!*

SOMEONE NEEDS TO TAKE OUT HIS BATTERIES!

I'M SORRY, EVERYONE. THERE'S JUST A LOT AT STAKE HERE. IF THIS PLAY'S A DUD, YOU MAY AS WELL SEND ME TO BELLEVUE AND HAVE ME *LOBOTOMIZED.*

I'M SURE IT'LL BE *FINE!*

HOW'D YOU GET THE IDEA FOR THIS ONE, ANY-HOW?

JOE LOUIS. REMEMBER HIM?

JOE LOUIS... LET ME THINK--

OF COURSE! HEAVYWEIGHT BOXER, A REAL POWERHOUSE.

HE'S ALL WASHED UP, FORCED TO DO WRESTLING SHOWS FOR A LIVING...

WHAT A SHAME.

THAT'S SHOWBIZ FOR YOU. ONE DAY YOU'RE ON TOP OF THE WORLD, THE NEXT, YOU'RE A JOKE-- FORGOTTEN, HUMILIATED, *DISCARDED.*

OH, ROD, LIGHTEN UP.

THERE! IT'S STARTING!

LIVE! FROM TELEVISION CITY IN HOLLYWOOD. *PLAYHOUSE 90,* BROUGHT TO YOU BY CAMEL, FAR AND AWAY THE WORLD'S LARGEST SELLING CIGARETTE.

PLAYHOUSE 90

THE DOC SAYS YOU'VE HAD IT. NO MORE! SAYS YOU GOTTA LEAVE NOW.

SO WHAT'LL I DO?

WELL, I DUNNO, YOU DO WHATEVER YOU WANNA DO! ANYTHING YOU LIKE! IT'S AS EASY AS THAT!

NO, NO, NO, NO! I MEAN A GUY'S GOTTA *DO SOMETHIN'!*

THEN DO SOMETHING!

BUT, MAISH, I DUNNO ANYTHIN' BUT FIGHTIN'!

THE PRODUCERS AND NETWORK LOVED "REQUIEM."
BUT IT WAS THE *PRESS* THAT WOULD MAKE OR BREAK IT.

HAVE YOU GOT THE NEW YORK TIMES YET?

WEREN'T YOU HERE JUST THIS MORNING?

YEAH, BUT I'M LOOKING FOR THE EVENING EDITION.

YOU'RE IN LUCK, CHUM.

DING!

IT WASN'T A DUD. IT WAS A KNOCK OUT *SUCCESS.* JACK GOULD, CRITIC OF THE NEW YORK TIMES *PRAISED* THE SHOW.

I HAD PROVEN TO THE WORLD THAT I WASN'T JUST SOME "ONE-TRICK PONY."

BUT DESPITE THE SUCCESS OF "REQUIEM," I STILL FELT FRUSTRATED. I WAS SICK OF FIGHTING CENSORS AND THE NETWORK OVER *EACH* AND *EVERY* SCRIPT.

ROD! FANCY SEEING YOU HERE!

SHALL WE JOIN FORCES?

THAT'S *STRANGE,* MRS. SORENSON IS USUALLY SO FRIENDLY.

DON'T FORGET, FRED, YOU'RE WALKING WITH A *JEW.*

DO YOU THINK THAT'S WHAT'S GOING ON?

I KNOW IT. NOT EVERYONE IS AS OPEN-MINDED AS YOU ARE.

THEY'RE WONDERING WHAT *I'M* DOING IN *THEIR* SQUEAKY-CLEAN CONNECTICUT NEIGHBORHOOD...

AND NOT IN THE *TENEMENTS,* WHERE I BELONG.

HEY, I SAW YOUR SHOW THE OTHER DAY, "THE ARENA"-- BOY, THAT WAS **GREAT!**

YOU'RE TOO KIND. FAR TOO KIND.

I THOUGHT IT WAS A FINE SHOW, BUT WHAT DO I KNOW.

IT COULD HAVE BEEN *INCREDIBLE.* BUT THE CENSORS AND THE SPONSORS...THEY *KILLED IT* BEFORE IT WAS BORN.

SEE-- I'M WRITING A *POLITICAL* DRAMA, BUT THE SENATORS CAN'T EVEN DISCUSS ANY *CURRENT ISSUES.*

ANYTHING EVEN *REMOTELY* RELATED TO THE POLITICAL SCENE IS *FORBIDDEN.*

THEY'RE TALKIN' HIEROGLYPHICS ABOUT MAKE-BELIEVE ISSUES.

BUT WASN'T THE *HEART* OF THE STORY STILL THERE?

I'M NOT SURE IT WAS. I'M WRITING IN A PRISON CELL, FRED, AND IT'S SHRINKING BY THE *DAY!*

I SWEAR TO YOU, IF I HAD WRITTEN "THE ARENA" AS SCIENCE FICTION....IF I HAD SET THE STORY IN THE YEAR 2057, AND PEOPLED THE SENATE WITH ROBOTS, I WOULD'VE HAD MUCH MORE FREEDOM.

SOON AFTER, I BEGAN TO SCOUR MY ARCHIVE.

IT WASN'T LONG BEFORE I FOUND WHAT I WAS LOOKING FOR...

AN OLD SCRIPT I HAD WRITTEN RIGHT AFTER COLLEGE.

IT WAS ONLY HALF AN HOUR, SO I KNEW I HAD TO EXPAND IT.

VIRGINIA, I WANT YOU TO TRANSCRIBE THIS FOR ME.

AND TYPE UP A TITLE PAGE.

THE TWILIGHT ZONE.

"THE TIME ELEMENT."

BY ROD SERLING.

THE TWILIGHT ZONE

The Time Element

By

Rod Serling

THIS WILL BE AN ANTHOLOGY SHOW, THE LIKES OF WHICH HAS NEVER BEEN SEEN BEFORE.

CBS

THIS IS NO *CAPTAIN VIDEO* OR *FLASH GORDON*--BUT RATHER, SHORT FILMS OF THE *HIGHEST* QUALITY!

YES, SCIENCE FICTION AND FANTASY, BUT DEALING WITH COMPLEX, ADULT ISSUES.

A SHOW WITH MORAL AND EMOTIONAL GRAVITY. DIRECTED BY THE VERY BEST, STARRING THE FINEST ACTORS.

VERY... *INTERESTING.*

CBS WAS CORDIAL, THEY EVEN BOUGHT THE SCRIPT.

THEY PROMISED ME THEY WOULD CONSIDER THE SHOW WITH THE *UTMOST* SINCERITY.

MARSHA, HAVE THIS FILED IN ROOM B404.

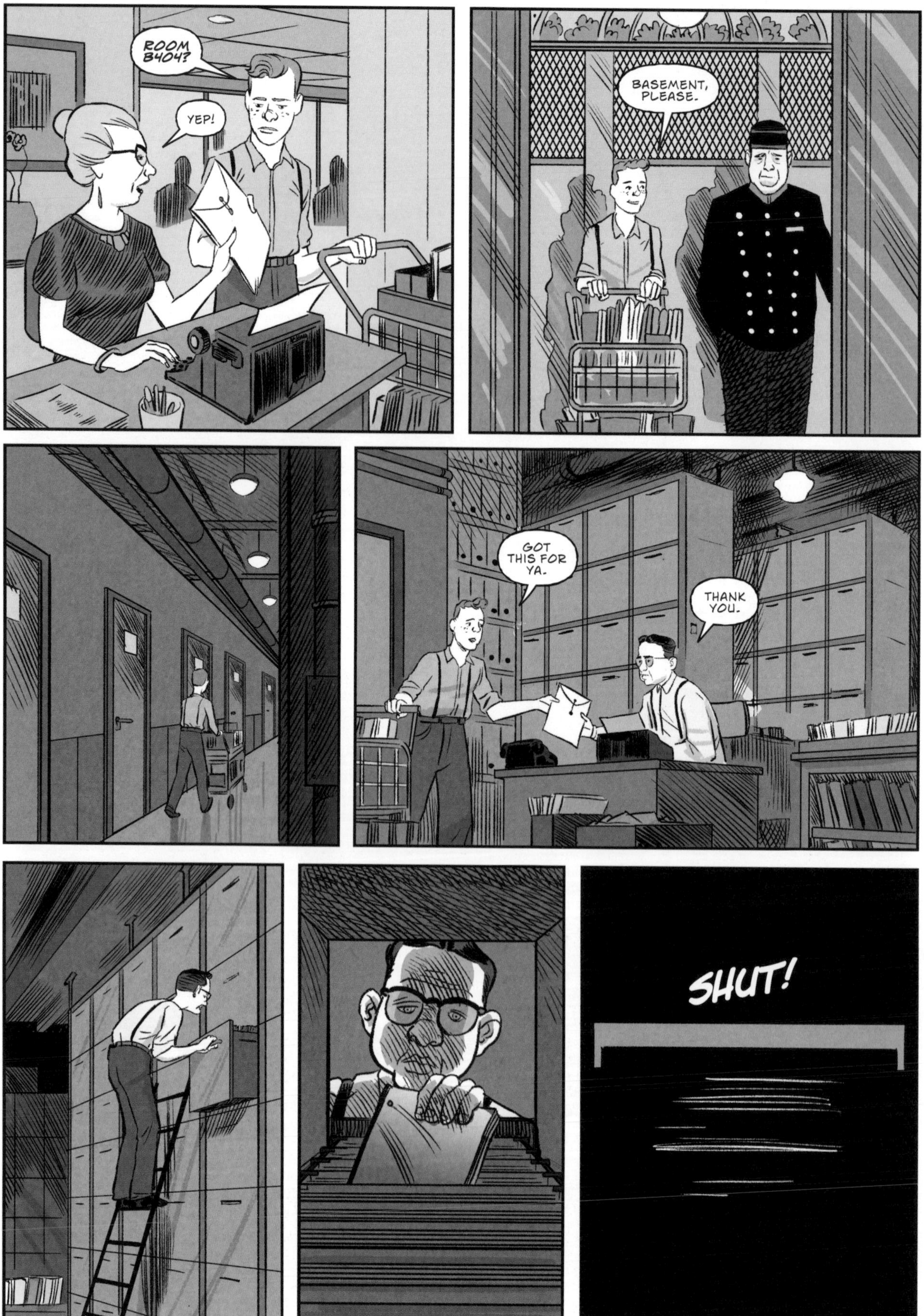
ROOM B404?
YEP!
BASEMENT, PLEASE.
GOT THIS FOR YA.
THANK YOU.
SHUT!

PART III

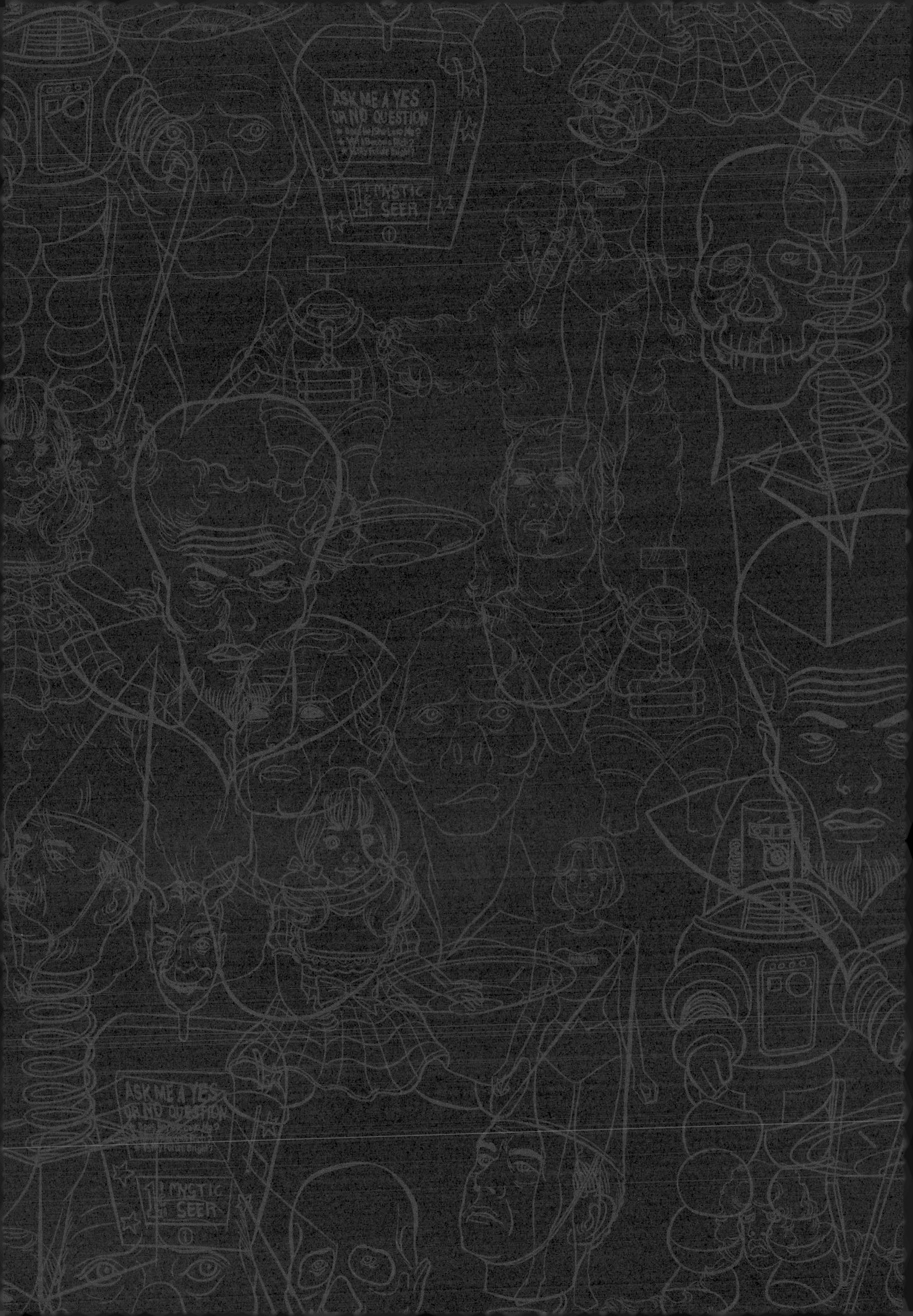
ASK ME A YES OR NO QUESTION
MYSTIC SEER
ASK ME A YES OR NO QUESTION
MYSTIC SEER

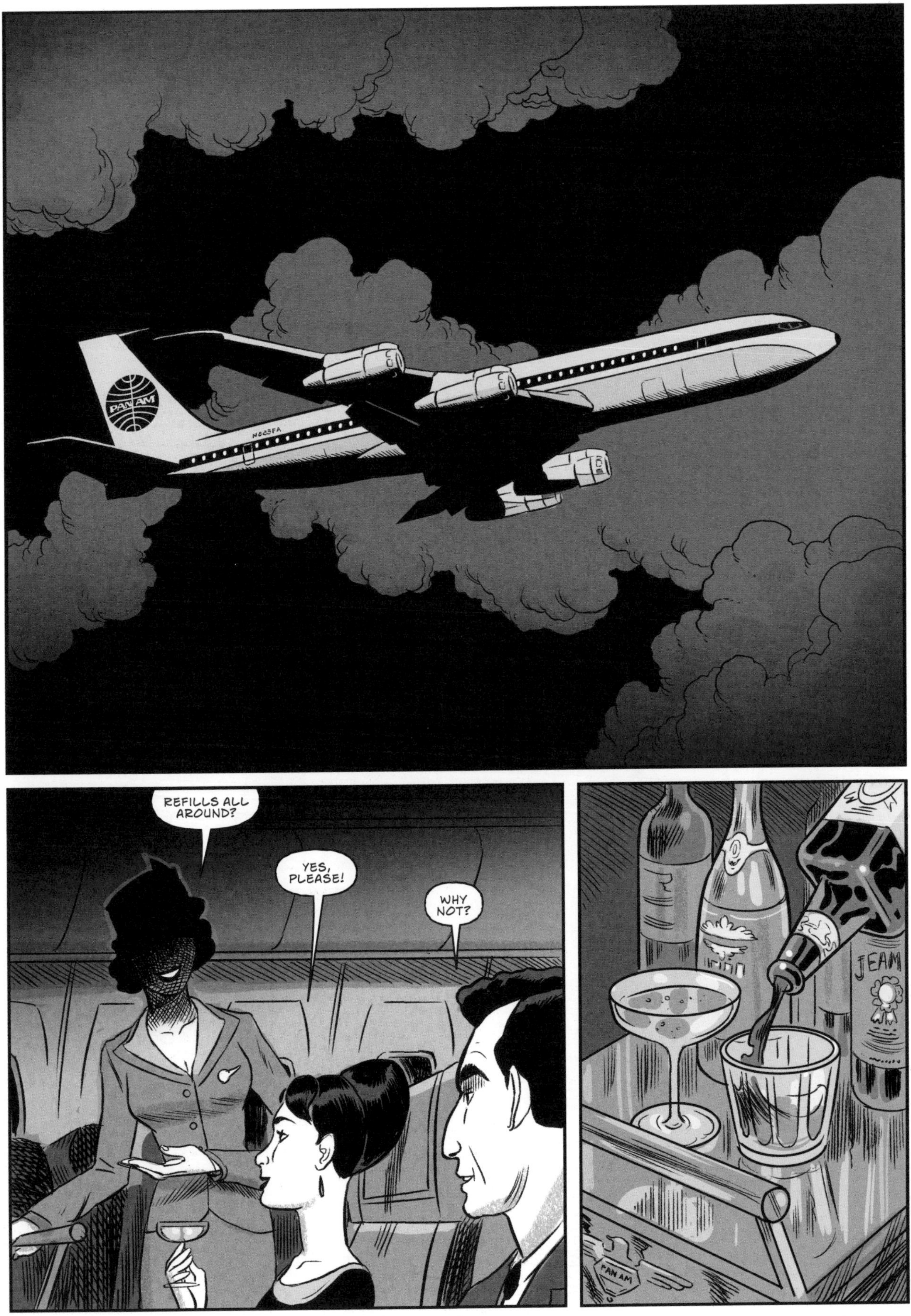
PAN AM
REFILLS ALL AROUND?
YES, PLEASE!
WHY NOT?
PAN AM

LOOK AT ME... GETTING CARRIED AWAY! I PROMISED MYSELF I WOULDN'T TALK ABOUT SHOW BUSINESS.

THAT'S QUITE ALL RIGHT, YOU DON'T HEAR ME COMPLAINING.

WHAT TIME IS IT?

I DON'T HAVE A WATCH. DOES IT *MATTER?* WE HAVE NOTHING *ELSE* TO DO.

THAT'S TRUE.

WELL, DON'T LEAVE ME HANGING, NOW! HOW DID IT ALL TURN OUT?

YOU'VE GOT A *LOVELY* SMILE, HAS ANYONE EVER TOLD YOU THAT?

QUIT STALLING!

HA, VERY WELL. WHERE WERE WE? THE SCRIPT REMAINED BURIED IN *CBS.* BUT I HAD OTHER WORRIES ON MY MIND. THE WINDS OF CHANGE WERE IN THE AIR.

TELEVISION WAS RAPIDLY LEAVING NEW YORK AND MOVING WEST. IN HOLLYWOOD, THE WHOLE TENOR OF THE MEDIUM SHIFTED.

THE TRADITIONAL LIVE ANTHOLOGY SHOWS BEGAN DROPPING DEAD LEFT AND RIGHT.

I HAD TO MOVE ON WITH THE TIMES....OR *PERISH.*

BY LATE '57, I HAD BECOME A PROUD RESIDENT OF *THE CITY OF LOS ANGELES*...

WITH A NINE-BEDROOM MANSION IN THE PACIFIC PALISADES, COMPLETE WITH A TENNIS COURT, POOL...

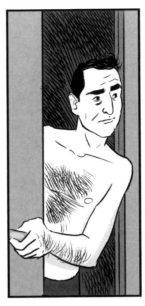

...AND ALL OTHER *TRAPPINGS* OF A SUCCESSFUL HOLLYWOOD WRITER.

CLICK

BUBBLELAND, AS I LIKED TO CALL IT, HAD GOTTEN TO ME FASTER THAN A PIRANHA AFTER A BLEEDING LIMB.

YOU KNOW HOW THEY DO IT, ERNIE?

THEY GIVE YOU A THOUSAND DOLLARS A WEEK...

...AND THEY *KEEP ON* GIVING YOU A THOUSAND DOLLARS A WEEK UNTIL THAT'S WHAT YOU *NEED* TO LIVE ON.

"AND AFTER THAT..."

"...YOU LIVE EVERY DAY AFRAID THAT THEY'LL TAKE IT AWAY FROM YOU."*

*"THE VELVET ALLEY," PLAYHOUSE 90

TAKE GOOD CARE OF HER, SKIP!

OF COURSE, MR. SERLING.

BERT! IT'S SUCH A PLEASURE TO FINALLY MEET YOU!

THE PLEASURE IS *ALL MINE,* ROD.

LOOK AT YOU! I WAS EXPECTING AN ANXIOUS NEW YORK PLAYWRIGHT IN A TWEED JACKET, AND INSTEAD I GET A MEETING WITH *MR. HOLLYWOOD!*

WHAT CAN I SAY? I THOUGHT I'D HATE IT HERE. TURNS OUT--I KINDA LIKE IT. YOU SHOULD SEE MY CONVERTIBLE!

YOU'RE PREACHING TO THE CHOIR, ROD.

LATER.

ANOTHER ROUND?

HOW COULD WE SAY "NO" TO YOU?

OKAY, I'D BETTER GET ON WITH IT, BEFORE I GET TOO DRUNK.

I'M GOING TO BE THE FIRST TO TELL YOU, DESILU PLAYHOUSE* HAS BEEN A TOUGH NUT FOR ME TO CRACK.

HOW DO YOU LEND *PRESTIGE* TO AN UNPRETENTIOUS SHOW, HOSTED BY A WACKY COUPLE?

I DON'T KNOW. HOW *DO* YOU?

TWO THINGS: ONE, YOU HIRE THE BEST GODDAMN *ACTORS* IN TOWN.

TWO, YOU HIRE THE BEST DAMN *SCREENWRITERS* IN TOWN--

AND I'M ASSUMING THAT'S WHERE *I* COME IN.

CORRECT.

I WOULD *LOVE* TO CONTRIBUTE, BUT I'M FULLY COMMITED FOR THE FORSEEABLE FUTURE. I SHOULD COME UP FOR AIR SOMETIME IN THE YEAR *2000.*

I SEE. IS THERE ANYTHING *UNPRODUCED* LYING AROUND IN ONE OF YOUR FILE CABINETS?

THINK-- THERE MUST BE *SOMETHING* OUT THERE.

HMMM. THERE IS *ONE* THING. IF I'M NOT MISTAKEN, I SOLD SOMETHING TO CBS IN '57. IT WAS TOO *"OUT THERE"* FOR THEM, SO THEY SHELVED IT.

*AN ANTHOLOGY SHOW PRODUCED BY LUCILLE BALL AND DESI ARNAZ.

GRANET WASTED NO TIME.

HE WENT OUT TO CBS AND BOUGHT OUT MY SCRIPT FOR THE HIGH SUM OF **$10,000.**

THE SCRIPT WAS ADDED TO THE PRODUCTION SCHEDULE, BUT IMMEDIATELY ENCOUNTERED RESISTANCE FROM McCANN-ERICKSON, THE AGENCY REPRESENTING THE SHOW'S SPONSORS.

THIS IS AN ABSOLUTE FIRM *NO* FROM US, BRET.

I'M MAKING THIS SHOW *HAPPEN!* YOU PROMISED ME CONTROL OVER CONTENT!

McCANN-ERICKSON WENT AS FAR AS FLYING SOME SUITS TO LA IN AN ATTEMPT TO PERSUADE GRANET TO DROP THE WHOLE THING.

PEARL HARBOR IS STILL A *TOUCHY* SUBJECT!

AND WHAT'S WITH THAT STRANGE ENDING? IT'S TOO *AVANT-GARDE.*

VIEWERS WILL GET CONFUSED.

LISTEN GUYS, I LIKE IT. THERE'S NOTHING TO BE CONFUSED ABOUT: IT'S A FUN PIECE OF *ENTERTAINMENT!*

STOP BEING AFRAID OF YOUR OWN SHADOW.

THERE WAS NO ARGUING WITH DESI ARNAZ.

YOU *HEARD* THE MAN.

ROD, I HAVE GOOD NEWS FOR YOU. AFTER A SERIOUS UPHILL BATTLE, I MANAGED TO GREENLIGHT "THE TIME ELEMENT"!

McCANN-ERICKSON SWORE TO GRANET THAT HE'D NEVER PRODUCE ANOTHER SCIENCE-FICTION SHOW AGAIN.

"THE TIME ELEMENT" FINALLY AIRED ON NOVEMBER 24TH, 1958, AS PART OF DESILU PLAYHOUSE.

THE EPISODE TELLS THE STORY OF ONE *PETER JENSON*, WHO IS SENT BACK IN TIME TO DECEMBER 1941 AND TRIES TO WARN PEOPLE ABOUT THE UPCOMING JAPANESE ATTACK ON PEARL HARBOR.

THE TIME ELEMENT

I KNOW WHAT'S GONNA HAPPEN TOMORROW! 'CAUSE TOMORROW IS DECEMBER 7TH, 1941 TO *YOU* PEOPLE, BUT IT'S *SEVENTEEN YEARS AGO* TO ME!

I'M TELLING YOU THAT TOMORROW *MORNING,* WE'RE GONNA GET *ATTACKED!*

I TOLD YOU! I TOLD YOU! I TOLD YOU!

WHY WOULDN'T ANYONE LISTEN TO ME??

AFTER THE EPISODE AIRED, CBS WAS FLOODED WITH OVER *SIX THOUSAND LETTERS* FROM VIEWERS WHO *LOVED* THE "THE TIME ELEMENT."

the Time Element
Hypnotic And Fresh

THE SHOW DEL... PRIS...
POWERFUL WRITING B...
AND A CAS...

AND REVIEWS WERE ALL-AROUND POSITIVE.

CBS REALIZED THE MISTAKE THEY'D MADE BY SHELVING MY PITCH. SUDDENLY THEY WERE READY TO DISCUSS *THE TWILIGHT ZONE.*

GET AHOLD OF ROD SERLING FOR ME.

W. DOZIER

SINCE "THE TIME ELEMENT" WAS USED ON *DESILU PLAYHOUSE,* I WAS ASKED TO COME UP WITH A *NEW* PILOT SCRIPT.

SO WE BOTH READ "THE HAPPY PLACE."

AND?

WELL, ROD, HOW DO I PUT THIS. IT'S SIMPLY *TOO DARK* FOR A PILOT.

THE SPONSORS ARE *NOT* GOING TO STAND BEHIND A SCRIPT ABOUT *EUTHANASIA!*

IT'S DOWNBEAT AND DEPRESSING. WE CAN'T LAUNCH A SHOW ON SUCH A MORBID NOTE.

I HOPE YOU UNDERSTAND, AND THAT THIS DOESN'T UPSET YOU...

UPSET? NO, NOT AT ALL!

I HAVE A WHOLE DRAWER *FULL* OF IDEAS!

I'LL JUST WRITE A *NEW* PILOT.

AND SO I DID.

THE CONCEPT FOR "WHERE IS EVERYBODY" CAME TO ME WHILE WALKING THROUGH THE EMPTY LOT OF A MOVIE STUDIO.

THE PLOT DEALT WITH AN AMNESIAC WALKING THROUGH AN ABANDONED TOWN IN SEARCH OF PEOPLE. WE ULTIMATELY DISCOVER THAT HE HAS BEEN HALLUCINATING THE WHOLE TIME, AS RESULT OF AN ARMY ISOLATION EXPERIMENT.

THE PREMISE WAS SIMPLE AND STRAIGHTFORWARD. IT WOULDN'T *SCARE* ANY SPONSORS.

I'M SORRY, OLD BUDDY. I DON'T RECOLLECT THE NAME.

THE FACE IS VAGUELY FAMILIAR, BUT THE NAME ESCAPES ME.

Soda 30¢

Banana Split 40¢

PLEASE, SOMEBODY *HELP ME!*

SOMEBODY HELP ME, SOMEBODY'S *WATCHING ME!*

"UP THERE, UP THERE IN THE VASTNESS OF SPACE, IN THE VOID THAT IS SKY...UP THERE IS AN ENEMY KNOWN AS *ISOLATION.* IT SITS THERE IN THE STARS, WAITING, WAITING WITH THE PATIENCE OF EONS, FOREVER WAITING....*IN THE TWILIGHT ZONE.*"

CBS FLEW ME OUT TO NEW YORK TO TRY TO SEDUCE SOME SPONSORS. I WAS ARMED WITH A REEL OF THE PILOT AND A SHORT INTRO I'D PREPARED SPECIALLY FOR THE OCCASION.

WELL GENTLEMEN, WITHOUT FURTHER ADO...

HOW D'YOU DO? YOU GENTLEMEN, OF COURSE, KNOW HOW TO *PUSH* A PRODUCT. THAT, ESSENTIALLY, IS YOUR *JOB.* MY PRESENCE HERE IS FOR MUCH THE SAME PURPOSE, TO *PUSH A PRODUCT!*

TO ACQUAINT YOU WITH AN ENTERTAINMENT PRODUCT WHICH WE HOPE, AND WHICH WE RATHER *EXPECT,* WILL MAKE YOUR PRODUCT-PUSHING MUCH EASIER.

WHAT YOU'RE ABOUT THE SEE, GENTLEMEN, IS A SERIES CALLED *THE TWILIGHT ZONE.* WE THINK IT'S A RATHER *SPECIAL* KIND OF SERIES. THIS IS A SERIES FOR THE STORYTELLING, SINCE IT IS OUR THINKING THAT AN AUDIENCE WILL ALWAYS SIT STILL AND LISTEN AND WATCH A *WELL-TOLD* STORY.

NOW THAT I'VE *IMMODESTLY* GONE ON RECORD PREDICTING THE HIGH QUALITY OF THIS SERIES, LET ME BRIEFLY SHOW YOU WHAT I MEAN BY, "A SPECIAL KIND OF SHOW."

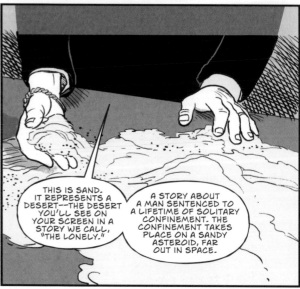

THIS IS SAND. IT REPRESENTS A DESERT--THE DESERT YOU'LL SEE ON YOUR SCREEN IN A STORY WE CALL, "THE LONELY."

A STORY ABOUT A MAN SENTENCED TO A LIFETIME OF SOLITARY CONFINEMENT. THE CONFINEMENT TAKES PLACE ON A SANDY ASTEROID, FAR OUT IN SPACE.

GENTLEMEN, I CAN ONLY TELL YOU THAT "THE LONELY," WHICH INVOLVES A MAN, AND A WOMAN MADE OUT OF PLASTIC AND WIRES WITH A MACHINE FOR A HEART, WILL PROVIDE A MOST *BIZARRE* EXPERIENCE.

OBJECT IN POINT HERE--A FILE CABINET CONTAINING A CONTRACT, ALL VERY LEGAL AND PROPER, EXCEPT, THE PARTY OF THE FIRST PART IN THIS CASE, WHAT DO WE CALL HIM? HE HAS A LOT OF NAMES. *BEELZEBUB, MR. SCRATCH.*

IN OUR STORY, "ESCAPE CLAUSE," HIS NAME IS SIMPLY *MR. CADWALLADER.*

HE MAKES A *DEAL* WITH A LITTLE MAN WHO HAS A PSYCHOTIC FEAR OF DYING.

MR. CADWALLADER SUPPLIES THE IMMORTALITY, AND THE LITTLE MAN SUPPLIES THE *SOUL.*

MY PITCH WAS A *SUCCESS.* WE LANDED KIMBERLY CLARK AND GENERAL FOODS AS SPONSORS.

A CONTRACT WAS DRAWN OUT. I WOULD RETAIN *COMPLETE CREATIVE CONTROL* OVER THE SHOW.

I WOULD WRITE 80% OF THE FIRST SEASON'S SCRIPTS AND IN RETURN, OWN A 50% STAKE IN THE SHOW. I COULDN'T HAVE IMAGINED A *BETTER* DEAL.

THE TWILIGHT ZONE WOULD BE PRODUCED BY MY NEWLY FORMED PRODUCTION COMPANY, CAYUGA PRODUCTIONS*.

*AFTER CAYUGA LAKE, NEW YORK, WHERE THE SERLINGS VACATIONED.

WELCOME TO Fabulous LAS VEGAS NEVADA

TO CELEBRATE THE NEWS, CAROL AND I WENT ON A LITTLE RETREAT.

Special Jackpot $10 000 00

DING DING! DING DING

YOU WON ALL THAT?

I DID. HOW ABOUT YOU, ANY LUCK?

NO, THIS MACHINE HAS ENSLAVED ME!

THEN JUST CUT YOUR LOSSES AND COME BACK TO THE ROOM, IT'S GETTING LATE!

IN A BIT, HONEY, I JUST NEED A LITTLE MORE TIME TO GET MY DAMN MONEY BACK FROM THIS MECHANICAL BASTARD.

SUIT YOURSELF.

I SWEAR THAT MACHINE WAS DEMONIC. I ALMOST LOST MY PANTS THAT NIGHT, BUT AT LEAST IT GAVE ME A GOOD IDEA FOR A STORY.

OL-A-TOP

THE TWILIGHT ZONE WAS THE RESULT OF THE STRANGE CONCOCTION OF ELEMENTS BREWING IN MY *SUBCONSCIOUS.*

AS I AWOKE FROM MY NIGHTLY TERRORS, IDEAS WOULD SURFACE UP, AND I WOULD JOT THEM DOWN.

ARMY MEMORIES

HORROR FILMS

BOOKS BY HEINLEIN, LOVECRAFT AND BRADBURY

NORMAN CORWIN BROADCASTS

TWISTED AND TRANSMUTED BY MY *OWN* IMAGINATION...

...THAT WAS THE STRANGE BREW THAT BECAME *THE TWILIGHT ZONE.*

AS SOON AS THE SHOW WAS GREENLIT, I REALIZED WITH CERTAIN PANIC THAT I WAS *OUT OF MY ELEMENT.*

DING DONG

SURE, I USED TO READ *AMAZING STORIES* AS A KID, BUT IT'D BEEN YEARS SINCE I DIPPED INTO THE GENRE.

I NEEDED SOMEONE WHO WAS AN *EXPERT* IN THE MEDIUM.

I REACHED OUT TO *RAY BRADBURY,* WHO I GREATLY ADMIRED.

COME IN, COME IN!

I HAVE TO APOLOGIZE IN ADVANCE FOR MY IGNORANCE, RAY, I'M A JOHNNY-COME-LATELY WHEN IT COMES TO LITERATURE OF THE FANTASTIC.

THAT'S QUITE ALL RIGHT, YOU'VE COME TO THE RIGHT PLACE.

THESE ARE EXCITING TIMES IN OUR FIELD. THERE'S A WEALTH OF INCREDIBLE MATERIAL.

HERE, THIS IS AN OUTSTANDING ANTHOLOGY BY ONE OF MY PROTÉGÉS, *CHUCK BEAUMONT,* HE'S A REAL SPARKPLUG.

I'LL MAKE SURE TO INTRODUCE YOU TO HIM SOON.

AND YOU *MUST* READ THESE TWO BY *RICK MATHESON,* ANOTHER YOUNG TALENTED MAN WHO I'VE BEEN MENTORING.

OH, AND YOU *ABSOLUTELY* MUST READ TOM'S A-COLD BY *JOHN COLLIER.*

BRILLIANT, SIMPLY BRILLIANT!

RAY, HAVE YOU GIVEN SOME MORE THOUGHT TO WRITING A SCRIPT FOR THE SHOW? IT WOULD BE SUCH AN HONOR TO HAVE YOU ON BOARD.

HMM, YES... YES, WHY NOT? I'M ASSUMING YOU CAN BEAT *AMAZING STORIES'* FIVE-CENTS-A-WORD RATE?

THOUGH I DESPERATELY WANTED TO, IT WAS NOT HUMANLY POSSIBLE FOR ME TO WRITE EVERY SINGLE EPISODE OF THE SHOW--THAT'S WHERE PRODUCER *BUCK HOUGHTON* KICKED INTO GEAR AND BEGAN A SEARCH FOR CO-WRITERS.

RICHARD MATHESON WAS ALREADY A WELL-ESTABLISHED WRITER WHEN HE BEGAN TO WORK ON THE TWILIGHT ZONE.

HE HAD PUBLISHED SEVERAL NOVELS, INCLUDING *I AM LEGEND* AND *THE SHRINKING MAN*--BOTH OF WHICH WOULD BE ADAPTED INTO FILMS.

HE HAD SOME TELEVISION CREDITS UNDER HIS BELT AS WELL, HAVING WRITTEN FOR WESTERNS SUCH AS *HAVE GUN, WILL TRAVEL.*

WHILE WORKING ON *THE ZONE*, RICHARD ALSO ADAPTED FIVE WORKS OF EDGAR ALLAN POE FOR ROGER CORMAN.

INCLUDING "THE HOUSE OF USHER," "THE PIT AND THE PENDULUM," AND "THE RAVEN."

IN ALL, RICHARD WROTE SIXTEEN EPISODES OF *THE TWILIGHT ZONE*. SOME OF HIS MOST FAMOUS SCRIPTS WERE "NIGHTMARE AT 20,000 FEET" AND "STEEL."

BORN CHARLES LEROY NUTT AND RIDICULED FOR HIS LAST NAME, *CHUCK BEAUMONT* FOUND REFUGE IN READING SCIENCE FICTION AND FANTASY.

HIS SHORT STORIES--OFTEN DEALING WITH THE FANTASTIC--APPEARED IN *AMAZING STORIES* AND *PLAYBOY* MAGAZINE.

HE WOULD WRITE TWENTY-TWO EPISODES OF *THE TWILIGHT ZONE*, INCLUDING "THE HOWLING MAN," AN ADAPTATION OF HIS OWN SHORT STORY.

CHUCK GOT SICK TOWARDS THE END OF THE *TWILIGHT ZONE'S* RUN. HE QUICKLY LOST HIS ABILITY TO WRITE AND TELL STORIES.

HE WOULD DIE YOUNG, AT THE AGE OF THIRTY-EIGHT, AFTER WASTING AWAY FROM ALZHEIMER'S AND PICK'S DISEASE. WHEN HE DIED, HE LOOKED LIKE A NINETY-YEAR-OLD MAN.

IN THE FALL OF '59, I WENT ON A MEDIA TOUR TO PROMOTE THE DEBUT OF *THE TWILIGHT ZONE*...

MY LAST STOP WAS THE MIKE WALLACE SHOW.

THIS IS MIKE WALLACE WITH ANOTHER TELEVISION INTERVIEW IN OUR GALLERY OF COLORFUL PEOPLE. IN TELEVISION DRAMA, FEW NAMES HAVE THE PRESTIGE OF THAT OF OUR GUEST.

ROD SERLING IS THE *ONLY* WRITER TO HAVE WON *THREE* EMMY AWARDS, FOR "REQUIEM FOR A HEAVYWEIGHT," "PATTERNS" AND "THE COMEDIAN." WE'LL TALK TO HIM ABOUT CENSORSHIP IN TELEVISION, HIS FIGHT TO SAY WHAT HE BELIEVES, AND WE'LL LEARN WHAT HE MEANS BY "THE PRICE TAG THAT HANGS ON SUCCESS."

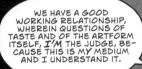

The MIKE WALLACE Interview

YOU'VE GOT A NEW SERIES COMING UP CALLED THE TWILIGHT ZONE. YOU'RE WRITING, AS WELL AS ACTING AS EXECUTIVE PRODUCER, ON THIS ONE. WHO CONTROLS THE FINAL PRODUCT: *YOU OR THE SPONSOR?*

WE HAVE A GOOD WORKING RELATIONSHIP, WHEREIN QUESTIONS OF TASTE AND OF THE ARTFORM ITSELF, *I'M* THE JUDGE, BE-CAUSE THIS IS *MY* MEDIUM AND I UNDERSTAND IT.

I'M A DRAMATIST FOR TELEVISION.

THIS IS THE AREA *I KNOW.*

I'VE BEEN TRAINED FOR IT. I'VE WORKED FOR AND IN IT FOR TWELVE YEARS, AND THE SPONSOR KNOWS HIS PRODUCT BUT HE DOESN'T KNOW MINE. SO WHEN IT COMES TO THE COMMERCIALS, I LEAVE THAT UP TO HIM. WHEN IT COMES TO THE STORY CONTENT, HE LEAVES IT UP TO ME.

IS PRE-CENSORSHIP* INVOLVED? ARE YOU SIMPLY WRITING EASY?

IN THIS PARTICULAR AREA, NO, BECAUSE WE'RE DEALING WITH A HALF-HOUR SHOW WHICH CANNOT PROBE LIKE A NINETY, WHICH DOESN'T USE SCRIPTS AS VEHICLES FOR SOCIAL CRITICISM. THESE ARE STRICTLY FOR ENTERTAINMENT.

THESE ARE POTBOILERS.**

OH, NO. I WOULDN'T CALL THEM "POTBOILERS" AT ALL. NO, THESE ARE VERY ADULT, HIGH-QUALITY, HALF-HOUR, EXTREMELY POLISHED FILMS.

BUT BECAUSE THEY DEAL IN THE AREAS OF FANTASY AND IMAGINATION AND SCIENCE FICTION, THERE'S NO OPPORTUNITY TO COP A PLEA OR CHOP AN AXE OR ANYTHING.

SO, IN ESSENCE, FOR THE TIME BEING AND FOR THE FORESEEABLE FUTURE, YOU'VE GIVEN UP ON WRITING ANYTHING IMPORTANT FOR TELEVISION, RIGHT?

WELL, AGAIN, THIS IS A SEMANTIC THING-- "IMPORTANT FOR TELEVISION"? I DON'T KNOW.

IF BY NOT IMPORTANT, YOU MEAN I'M NOT GOING TO TRY TO DELVE INTO CURRENT SOCIAL PROBLEMS DRAMATICALLY, YOU'RE QUITE RIGHT. I'M NOT.

*A TERM DISCUSSED BY TELEVISION PLAYWRIGHT PADDY CHAYEFSKY: THE PRACTICE OF A WRITER CENSORING HIS OR HER OWN WORK IN ANTICIPATION OF THE NETWORK AND/OR SPONSORS' FUTURE RESISTANCE

**A BOOK, PAINTING, OR RECORDING PRODUCED MERELY TO MAKE A LIVING BY CATERING TO POPULAR TASTE

ROD, **HERBERT BRODKIN**, A TV PRODUCER ASSOCIATED WITH SOME OF YOUR EARLIER PLAYS, HAS SAID THIS ABOUT YOU: "ROD IS EITHER GOING TO STAY COMMERCIAL OR BECOME A DISCERNING ARTIST, BUT **NOT BOTH.**"

NOW, HAS IT EVER OCCURRED TO YOU THAT YOU'RE SELLING YOURSELF **SHORT** BY TAKING ON A SERIES WHICH, BY YOUR **OWN** ADMISSION, IS GOING TO BE A SERIES PRIMARILY DESIGNED TO **ENTERTAIN?**

I PRESUME HERB MEANS THAT INHERENTLY YOU CANNOT BE COMMERCIAL **AND** ARTISTIC. YOU CANNOT BE COMMERCIAL **AND** OFFER QUALITY.

YOU CANNOT BE COMMERCIAL CONCURRENT WITH HAVING A PREOCCUPATION WITH THE LEVEL OF STORYTELLING THAT YOU WANT TO ACHIEVE. AND **THIS** I HAVE TO **REJECT.**

I THINK YOU **CAN** BE. I DON'T THINK CALLING SOMETHING "COMMERCIAL" TAGS IT WITH A KIND OF ODIOUS SUGGESTION THAT IT STINKS, THAT IT'S SOMETHING RAUNCHY TO BE **ASHAMED** OF.

HOW MANY HOURS A DAY DO YOU WORK RIGHT NOW AS EXECUTIVE PRODUCER AND/ OR WRITER ON THE TWILIGHT ZONE?

TWELVE TO FOURTEEN HOURS A DAY.

HOW MANY DAYS A WEEK?

SEVEN.

I'M NOT ASKING FOR FIGURES HERE, BUT OBVIOUSLY THE TWILIGHT ZONE IS YOUR OWN CREATION. I THINK THAT OUR AUDIENCE WOULD BE FASCINATED TO KNOW, HOW RICH CAN A FELLOW GET UNDER THESE CIRCUMSTANCES?

WELL, IF THE SHOW IS SUCCESSFUL, HE CAN GET **TREMENDOUSLY** RICH.

121

AND SO THE GRIND BEGAN. I HAD TO COME UP WITH TWENTY-SEVEN TELEPLAYS FOR THE UPCOMING SEASON.

I WOULD WAKE UP AT DAWN EVERY MORNING AND HEAD INTO THE HOME OFFICE.

I WAS WRITING FASTER THAN EVER BEFORE. IT WAS THE KIND OF SCHEDULE THAT IF I DROPPED A PENCIL AND BENT OVER TO PICK IT UP, I WAS TWO WEEKS BEHIND.

FATE'S THE NAME, HENRY J. FATE. AND YOU ARE AL DENTON, AND YOU'RE RUNNING AWAY. YOU SHOULDN'T, YOU KNOW... YOU SHOULDN'T RUN AWAY.

I SHOULDN'T? YEAH, I GUESS YOU'RE RIGHT. I SHOULDN'T RUN AWAY, I SHOULD STAY HERE AND GET *SHOT TO DEATH!*

EVERY DAY AROUND NOON, WHEN I COULDN'T WRITE ANYMORE, I WOULD HEAD TO THE STUDIO.

METRO-GOLDWYN-MAYER-STUDIOS

BEING THE SUPERVISING PRODUCER, I WANTED TO BE FULLY INVOLVED IN THE *MAKING* OF THE SHOW.

AT NIGHT, I WOULD DRAG MYSELF HOME, AND PROMPTLY CRASH.

ON OCTOBER 2ND, 1959, THE NORTHERN UNITED STATES WOULD WITNESS A FULL *SOLAR ECLIPSE.*

THAT EVENING, THE AMERICAN AUDIENCE WOULD BE INTRODUCED TO A SHOW THE LIKES OF WHICH NO ONE HAD EVER SEEN BEFORE.

VIEWERS WOULD--FOR THE FIRST TIME EVER--HEAR THAT UNCANNY THEME COMPOSED BY *BERNARD HERRMANN*...

...WHILE A SERIES OF BIZARRE SYMBOLS FLOATED ACROSS THEIR SCREENS.

"THERE IS A FIFTH DIMENSION, BEYOND THAT WHICH IS KNOWN TO MAN. IT IS A DIMENSION AS VAST AS SPACE, AND AS TIMELESS AS INFINITY.

"IT IS THE MIDDLE GROUND BETWEEN LIGHT AND SHADOW, BETWEEN SCIENCE AND SUPERSTITION...

"...AND IT LIES BETWEEN THE PIT OF MAN'S FEARS, AND THE SUMMIT OF HIS KNOWLEDGE.

"THIS IS THE DIMENSION OF IMAGINATION. IT IS AN AREA WHICH WE CALL..."

The TWILIGHT ZONE

WRITER'S ROOM

YOU GOT THE NUMBERS, *BUCK?*

THE SHOW WAS OFF TO A ROCKY START. DESPITE GETTING GOOD PRESS, THE FIRST EPISODE RECEIVED SUB-PAR RATINGS.

THINGS GOT WORSE BEFORE THEY GOT BETTER.

DO YOU *REALLY* WANT TO KNOW?

COME ON, HIT ME WITH IT. YOU KNOW I'M A BIG BOY.

16.3 ON NIELSEN.

AHHH! TAKE THE DAGGER OUT!

SERIOUSLY, ROD, HOW CAN WE COMPETE WITH *77 SUNSET STRIP**?

OUR DAYS ARE NUMBERED. I HEAR WAGON TRAIN IS HIRING, SHOULD I APPLY?

DON'T EULOGIZE THE SHOW QUITE YET. IT'S STILL EARLY IN THE GAME.

ALSO-- YOU'RE GOING TO *LIKE* THIS--

WE'VE BEEN GETTING QUITE A LOT OF LETTERS FROM TICKED-OFF PARENTS.

PARENTS?

THAT'S RIGHT. ASKING US TO PUT THE SHOW ON AT AN *EARLIER* TIME SLOT. APPARENTLY, THEIR KIDS ARE SNEAKING OUT OF BED TO WATCH IT!

*A DETECTIVE SHOW RUNNING ON ABC AT THE SAME TIME SLOT AS *THE TWILIGHT ZONE.*

THROUGHOUT ITS TENURE, THE SHOW WOULD NEVER BECOME A RATINGS TRIUMPH, BUT IT SLOWLY GATHERED A SIGNIFICANT GROUP OF *LOYAL FOLLOWERS.*

MEANWHILE, THE CRITICAL RESPONSE, HIGH PRODUCTION QUALITY AND UNUSUAL SUBJECT MATTER STARTED GENERATING SOME *HEAT* AROUND HOLLYWOOD.

HIGH-CALIBER ACTORS AND DIRECTORS WOULD ROUTINELY REQUEST TO ENTER "THE ZONE."

HO LLY W OOD

CAROL BURNETT

DENNIS HOPPER

ROBERT REDFORD

BUSTER KEATON

DON RICKLES

GEORGE TAKEI

WILLIAM SHATNER

JULIE NEWMAR

JACQUES TOURNEUR

IDA LUPINO

RICHARD DONNER

DON SIEGEL

MY PREDICTION CAME TRUE: BOTH SPONSORS AND CENSORS LEFT ME TO MY OWN DEVICES.

MAPLE STREET 300

THEY SAW NOTHING PROBLEMATIC WITH A SHOW DEALING WITH *ALIENS* AND *MONSTERS,* SOMEWHERE OFF IN THE *DISTANT* FUTURE.

I WOULD BURROW INTO THE DEEPEST, *DARKEST* RECESSES OF AMERICA'S SUBCONSCIOUS...

...HARVEST DARK MATTER, RESHAPE IT, DISGUISE IT, AND *SERVE IT BACK* TO THE MASSES.

WE'RE ROLLING!

THE TWILIGHT ZONE

SCENE 1   TAKE 1

DATE 5/4/59   SOUND

DIRECTOR Ronald Winston

WHAT *WAS* THAT? A METEOR?

MAYBE THERE'S A FAMILY THAT ISN'T WHAT WE THINK THEY ARE--MONSTERS FROM OUTER SPACE OR SOMETHING, FIFTH COLONISTS FROM THE *VAST BEYOND.*

NOW, DO YOU KNOW ANYBODY THAT MIGHT FIT THAT DESCRIPTION ON MAPLE STREET?

WHAT IS THIS, A PRACTICAL *JOKE* OR SOMETHING?

THE NATION WAS IN THE GRIPS OF A WAVE OF *PARANOIA.* THE AIR WAS THICK WITH FEAR AND DISTRUST... THE PUTRID SCENT OF McCARTHYISM.

I WAS OUTRAGED WITH WHERE WE WERE HEADED AS *PEOPLE.*

BIGOTRY, TOTALITARIANISM, WAR.

WE KNOW THAT THERE MUST BE A SINGLE PURPOSE, A SINGLE NORM, A SINGLE APPROACH, A SINGLE ENTITY OF PEOPLE, A SINGLE VIRTUE, A SINGLE MORALITY!

SOME DAYS, I FELT LIKE HUMANITY WAS ON THE BRINK OF *SELF-ANNIHILATION.*

IN THE ZONE--HIDDEN IN PLAIN SIGHT--I WAS ABLE TO EXPRESS MY DEEPEST ANXIETIES AND FRUSTRATIONS.

THEY'RE ALL DEAD! THEY MUST BE.

EVERYBODY'S DEAD!

I'M SURE I'LL BE FORGIVEN... THE WAY THINGS ARE.

EVEN THOUGH THE SHOW'S PROSPECTS WERE IMPROVING, I WAS SINKING DEEPER AND DEEPER INTO AN ABYSS OF DEPRESSION AND ANXIETY OF MY OWN MAKING.

IN ADDITION TO WRITING TWENTY EPISODES AND PRODUCING THE SHOW, I HAD AGREED TO TAKE ON THE TASK OF WRITING A BOOK OF SHORT STORIES.

MEANWHILE, I ALSO MANAGED TO SQUEEZE IN THREE NEW SCRIPTS FOR *PLAYHOUSE 90*.

... TO DIE FOR SOMETHING THAT YOU BELIEVE IN, THERE MUST BE PRIDE IN THIS.

ALL THE WHILE SUBSISTING ON COCA-COLA, COFFEE AND CIGARETTES.

I WAS UP TO FOUR PACKS A DAY.

I WAS IN CONSTANT FEAR OF *THE TWILIGHT ZONE* BEING CANCELED--SPONSORS COULD JUMP SHIP AT ANY MOMENT.

AGH!!!

WELL, YOUR BLOODWORK CAME IN.

EVERYTHING SEEMS TO BE IN ORDER.

YOUR BLOOD PRESSURE IS HIGHER THAN I WOULD *LIKE* IT TO BE, BUT OTHERWISE, NO RED FLAGS.

PERHAPS YOU MISSED SOMETHING?

I THOUGHT I WAS HAVING SOME SORT OF *CARDIAC* EPISODE.

NO, NO. YOU ARE SUFFERING FROM *ACUTE WORK FATIGUE.* YOU NEED TO TAKE A *BREAK.* PERHAPS A VACATION?

A BREAK IS OUT OF THE QUESTION, DOC. I'M RUNNING A WEEKLY SHOW! I HAVE COMMITMENTS.

VERY WELL. TRY TO GET MORE REST REGARDLESS. TAKE *NAPS* IN THE MIDDLE OF THE DAY.

I'M ALSO PRESCRIBING YOU A NEW TRANQUILIZER THAT JUST CAME ON THE MARKET, AND SOME SLEEPING PILLS TO COUNTER THE INSOMNIA.

AND *ROD...*

YES?

...TRY TO CUT DOWN ON THE SMOKING.

THE STRAINS OF WORK WERE ALSO MAKING THEIR WAY INTO THE FEW HOURS I'D SALVAGED FOR MY *FAMILY.*

WHAT WE NEED HERE, WILLIAMS, IS A SHOW WITH PIZZAZZ, AN ENTERTAINER WITH MOXY! WE'VE GOT TO SEIZE THE AUDIENCE FOR YEARS. GIVE THEM A *YANK!* JARR 'EM! ROCK 'EM! GIVE 'EM THE OL' *PUSH! PUSH! PUSH!*

I UNDERSTAND, MR. MISRELL.

NOW IT'S GOTTA BE BRIGHT, WILLIAMS, BRIGHT WITH...

I'M TRYING TO--

...COMEDY! IT'S GOTTA HAVE IT ALL! PUSH, PUSH, PUSH! NOW IT'S GOTTA BE BRIGHT, WILLIAMS! THIS IS A PUSH BUSINESS! *PUSH, PUSH, PUSH!*

THAT'S THE KIND OF SHOW THAT PEOPLE LIKE.

I UNDERSTAND MR. MISRELL, I UNDERSTAND. I'LL DO THE BEST I CAN.

DO MORE THAN YOU *CAN!* ASPIRE! DREAM BIG, THEN GET BEHIND IT! *PUSH, PUSH, PUSH!*

PUSH, PUSH, PUSH, WILLIAMS! PUSH, PUSH, PUSH!

CRACK!

ROD, WAKE UP!

WHAT? WHAT?

LOOK AT YOU, YOU CAN'T EVEN *STAY AWAKE* TO WATCH YOUR OWN SHOW.

IT'S BEEN A *ROUGH* WEEK.

I'M REALLY CONCERNED ABOUT YOU. THIS EPISODE WAS...SO DARK. THE AD EXEC, WILLIAMS, HE...HE COMMITS *SUICIDE!*

WELL, THAT'S OPEN TO INTERPRETATION.

AND THAT OTHER SCRIPT I READ, "A PASSAGE FOR TRUMPET." IT'S LIKE THE MAN HAS A *DEATH WISH.*

SO, WHAT'S THE PROBLEM?

I'M JUST REALLY *WORRIED* ABOUT YOU, I FEEL LIKE YOU'VE TAKEN ON TOO MUCH. WORK'S *GRINDING* YOU *DOWN.*

CAROL, YOU **KNOW** THIS INDUSTRY--IT'S FEAST OR FAMINE! I HAVE TO TAKE IT **ALL** IN WHILE THE TAKING IS **GOOD.**

I'M NOT GOING TO BE A "HOT COMMODITY" FOREVER.

PERHAPS, BUT DO YOU HAVE TO WRITE **THIS MANY** EPISODES? AND TAKE ON ALL THOSE OTHER PROJECTS?

IT'S TAKING A TOLL ON YOU, AND ON **US**... I...I REALLY FEEL LIKE WE'VE BEEN **DRIFTING APART.**

HONEY, I KNOW IT'S BEEN ROUGH, BUT I DON'T SEE ANY OTHER WAY--

THERE **ARE** OTHER WAYS. YOU NEED TO GET A LITTLE DISTANCE FROM YOUR WORK!

MY NAME IS ON THE **GODDAMN** SHOW! I'VE GIVEN YOU EVERYTHING!

LOOK AT THIS HOUSE, THIS POOL, THE JEWELRY, THE CLOTHES YOU WEAR! WHAT **ELSE** COULD YOU POSSIBLY **NEED?!**

DO I HAVE TO **SPELL IT OUT** FOR YOU? YOU'RE SPENDING MORE NIGHTS SLEEPING OUT IN THE OFFICE THAN IN **OUR** BED!

JESUS CHRIST, CAROL. I REALLY DON'T NEED MORE PRESSURE RIGHT NOW. I NEED YOU TO BE **SUPPORTIVE!**

OH ROD, I WISH YOU WOULD **WAKE UP** AND SEE WHAT YOU'VE BECOME.

ALL THE WHILE, A STORM WAS BREWING AT CBS...

AS PART OF A MAJOR NETWORK SHAKE UP IN '59, JAMES AUBREY-- A.K.A *"THE SMILING COBRA"*--WAS NAMED PRESIDENT, REPLACING LOUIS COWAN WHO WAS DISMISSED DUE TO THE QUIZ SHOW SCANDALS.*

SO YOU'RE TELLING ME A *SINGLE* EPISODE OF PLAYHOUSE 90 COSTS $175,000?

AUBREY'S ASCENT MARKED *THE END OF AN ERA.* HE WOULD CHANGE THE DIRECTION OF THE NETWORK AND OF THE MEDIUM AS A WHOLE. AUBREY'S MOTTO WAS "BROADS, BOSOMS, AND FUN."

WHY THE HELL ARE WE STILL PRODUCING THIS ELEPHANT?

HE WANTED HITS, AND IN ORDER TO HAVE THOSE HE WOULD APPEAL TO THE *LOWEST COMMON DENOMINATOR* WITH SHOWS LIKE *THE BEVERLY HILLBILLIES* AND *GILLIGAN'S ISLAND.*

IT'S MORE THAN JUST THE BOTTOM LINE WITH PLAYHOUSE 90, IT'S BEEN THE *GEM OF THE NETWORK* FOR YEARS.

IT LENDS US PRESTIGE!

YOU CAN'T BUY BUPKIS WITH *PRESTIGE.* I WANT A DETAILED COST ASSESSMENT VS. RETURNS ON MY DESK TOMORROW MORNING, *POST HASTE!*

YES, SIR.

VERY WELL, LET'S SEE WHO *ELSE* IS DRAINING OUR COFFERS. *AH! THE TWILIGHT ZONE!* WHAT A STRANGE, STRANGE SHOW. $65,000 AN EPISODE! *FOR HALF AN HOUR!* THAT'S OUTRAGEOUS.

AND SO BEGAN A TUG OF WAR BETWEEN THE NETWORK AND ME. DURING THE FOLLOWING SEASONS, AUBREY WOULD CHOP THE BUDGET DOWN *BIT BY BIT,* 'TIL THERE WAS ALMOST *NOTHING* LEFT.

*IN THE 1950S SEVERAL QUIZ SHOWS, SUCH AS *THE $64,000 QUESTION,* TURNED OUT TO BE RIGGED. CONTESTANTS WERE GIVEN THE ANSWERS AHEAD OF THE SHOW.

ONE OF AUBREY'S FIRST STABS AT US WAS DURING THE SECOND SEASON OF THE SHOW. IN AN ATTEMPT TO CUT COSTS WE WERE FORCED TO SHOOT SIX EPISODES ON *VIDEO* INSTEAD OF FILM.

AS MUST BE OBVIOUS, THIS IS A HOUSE HOVERED OVER BY *MR. DEATH,* THAT *OMNIPRESENT PLAYER* TO THE THIRD AND FINAL ACT OF EVERY LIFE. AND IT'S BEEN SAID, AND PROBABLY RIGHTFULLY SO--

--THAT WHAT FOLLOWS THIS LIFE IS ONE OF THE *UNFATHOMABLE* MYSTERIES, AN AREA OF DARKNESS WHICH WE, THE LIVING, RESERVE FOR THE DEAD--

FOR IN A MOMENT, A CHILD WILL TRY TO CROSS THAT BRIDGE WHICH SEPARATES LIGHT AND SHADOW, AND, OF COURSE, HE MUST TAKE THE ONLY KNOWN ROUTE, THAT INDISTINCT HIGHWAY THROUGH THE REGION WE CALL *THE TWILIGHT ZONE.*

THIS IS *AWFUL*, BUCK, AWFUL!

COME ON, ROD! IT'S NOT *THAT* BAD.

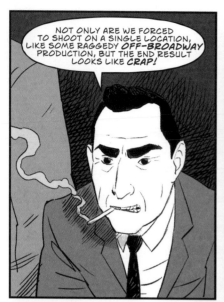

NOT ONLY ARE WE FORCED TO SHOOT ON A SINGLE LOCATION, LIKE SOME RAGGEDY *OFF-BROADWAY* PRODUCTION, BUT THE END RESULT LOOKS LIKE *CRAP!*

IT'S A NEW TECHNOLOGY.

BUT WHY DO *WE* HAVE TO BE THE GUINEA PIGS? HE'S *TAUNTING* US. I'M TELLING YOU. AUBREY PICKED THE *WRONG MAN* TO FIGHT WITH. I WON'T GO DOWN EASY.

CALM DOWN. I'VE TOLD THE NETWORK THE SAVINGS ARE MINUSCULE.

I'M PUSHING TO GET US BACK ON FILM.

IN THE END, VIDEO ONLY SAVED ABOUT $5,000 AN EPISODE, AND THE NETWORK AGREED TO TERMINATE THEIR COST-CUTTING EXPERIMENT.

AUBREY'S NEXT BLOW WAS EVEN *LOWER*— THE CANCELLATION OF *PLAYHOUSE 90.* THE PRODUCERS ASKED ME TO WRITE THE LAST EPISODE OF THE SHOW.

AND SO, IN THE SUMMER OF 1960, WE SHOT "IN THE PRESENCE OF MINE ENEMIES," STARRING A YOUNG *ROBERT REDFORD* IN ONE OF HIS FIRST TELEVISION ROLES.

WE'RE SURE TO REMEMBER THIS ONE, *HUH?*

ROD SERLING

FIELDER COOK

NO DOUBT ABOUT IT, FIELDER. I HOPE THE SOUND OF MY *SOBBING* DOESN'T *DROWN OUT* THE DIALOGUE.

I'VE ALREADY RUN OUT OF TEARS FROM THE REHEARSALS.

IT WAS A SCRIPT DEALING WITH THE *WARSAW GHETTO,* A SUBJECT SCARCELY EXPLORED ON TELEVISION OR FILM AT THAT POINT.

YOUNG SERGEANT LOTT, I'M GOING TO TALK ABOUT *MORALITY.*

THE MORALITY OF *HATING JEWS.*

REDFORD PLAYED A COMPASSIONATE NAZI OFFICER-- A STORYLINE WHICH SPARKED CONTROVERSY UPON BROADCAST. I WOULD LATER BE CRITICIZED FOR MY *HUMANE* DEPICTION OF A NAZI.

BUT THERE MUST BE AN *OBJECT* OF HATRED. SUDDENLY IN FRONT OF US, OUT STEPS A JEW. AN UNASSIMILATED *FOREIGNER* IN OUR MIDST. AND SO WE *HATE* IT, AND IN THE PROCESS, WE ARE *UNIFIED.*

BECAUSE THERE IS A MORALITY IN *HATING,* SERGEANT. IT HAPPENS TO BE A CLUE FOR SURVIVAL--NATIONS CAN *FEED* ON IT. THEY FIND THEIR STRENGTH IN IT. THEY ARE *NURTURED* BY IT, LOTT.

AFTER THE SHOOT WAS OVER, I LINGERED AROUND THE *EMPTY STUDIO*...

...WATCHING AS THE LAST BEACON OF OUR GOLDEN AGE DIMMED INTO *DARKNESS*.

EXIT

AS SEASON THREE OF *THE TWILIGHT ZONE* ROLLED IN, I BEGAN TO *RUN OUT* OF STEAM.

I'VE NEVER FELT QUITE AS DRAINED OF IDEAS AS I DID IN THAT MOMENT. STORIES USED TO BUBBLE OUT OF ME SO FAST, I COULDN'T GET THEM DOWN ON PAPER QUICK ENOUGH.
NO MORE.

I WAS WRITING SO MUCH, TO THE POINT WHERE I WASN'T ABLE TO RETAIN QUALITY IN MUCH OF THE WORK.

I BEGAN BORROWING FROM MYSELF. REPEATING MYSELF. MAKING MY OWN CLICHÉS.

THE PRESSURE WAS STARTING TO TAKE ITS TOLL IN OTHER DEPARTMENTS AS WELL.

LISTEN, ROD, I'VE TRIED TO KEEP THIS INSIDE AS LONG AS I COULD, BUT I JUST *CAN'T* ANYMORE.

YOU'VE BEEN *STEALING* FROM ME. AND NOT JUST ONCE, BUT OVER *SEVERAL* EPISODES!

CHUCK! WHAT *ON EARTH* ARE YOU TALKING ABOUT?

YOU KNOW *VERY WELL* WHAT I'M TALKING ABOUT!

I REALIZED I HAD INDEED BORROWED FROM BEAUMONT'S BOOKS IN SEVERAL EPISODES.

THAT NIGHT, I SENT HIM A LETTER OF APOLOGY.

ALL IS FORGIVEN. YOU'RE ALREADY PAYING ME MORE THAN ENOUGH TO WRITE ON THE SHOW. I MEAN, *WHO ELSE* IS MAKING THIS KIND OF MONEY WRITING SCIENCE-FICTION?

I'M GLAD. IT WON'T HAPPEN AGAIN, CHUCK!

I WAS WALKING A FINE LINE WITH BRADBURY AS WELL. HE WAS FRUSTRATED THAT WE WERE UNABLE TO PRODUCE HIS FIRST SCRIPT FOR US, "HERE THERE BE TYGERS."

WHEN WE FINALLY GOT HIS "I SING THE BODY ELECTRIC" MADE DURING THE THIRD SEASON, THERE WAS A *MAJOR SNAFU.*

MY FIRST FORAY INTO TELEVISION-- WILL THIS MARK THE BEGINNING OF MY DEMISE?

YOU'RE NOW A PART OF OUR SELL-OUT COVEN!

THIS CAN'T BE...

OH NO, THESE ARE JUST THE *BITS* AND *PIECES.* JUST THE EYES, THE LIPS, THE LIMBS FROM WHICH YOU WILL CHOOSE THE ELEMENTS THAT WILL BECOME--

OUR GRAND- MOTHER?

PREPOSTEROUS!

WHAT IS IT RAY?

WHY, THIS IS AN OUTRAGE! HE *CUT OUT* THE MOST *CRUCIAL* SCENE! HE PROMISED ME THEY WOULDN'T CHANGE MY SCRIPT! HE... HE *PROMISED!*

141

WITH *THE ZONE* ON THE BRINK OF CANCELLATION AND FUTURE INCOME UNCERTAIN, I MADE A MOVE I WOULD LATER DEEPLY REGRET.

I AGREED TO APPEAR IN A COMMERCIAL. IT PAID THREE GRAND FOR A FEW HOURS' WORK. I HOPED THAT THE AD WOULD COME AND GO UNNOTICED.

WE WILL RETURN TO THE EMMY CEREMONY AFTER THIS SHORT BREAK.

I'M SORRY YOU DIDN'T WIN, HONEY.

CAN'T WIN 'EM EVERY YEAR. IT WAS AN HONOR JUST TO BE--

LADIES AND GENTLEMEN, FIVE-TIME EMMY AWARD WINNER, *ROD SERLING!*

WHEN I WANT TO KICK BACK AND RELAX WITH A COLD BEER, THERE'S ONLY *ONE* BRAND THAT COMES TO MIND.

SCHLITZ, WITH SMOOTH FLAVOR AND FULL BODY!

real gusto

FOR A BEER WITH *REAL GUSTO*, CHOOSE SCHLITZ.

gusto

WOW!

HA!

HAHA!

DID YOU *SEE* THAT?

CAROL AND I HAD TO SNEAK OUT OF THE BUILDING.

IT WAS THE PERFECT TIME FOR AN ESCAPE FROM HOLLYWOOD.

DURING THE HIATUS BEFORE THE NEXT SEASON, I TOOK A SABBATICAL OF SORTS.

ONCE AGAIN, I WAS AT ANTIOCH COLLEGE IN YELLOW SPRINGS, OHIO--THIS TIME AS A VISITING INSTRUCTOR.

I'D BE LYING IF I SAID I DIDN'T EXPECT A ROYAL WELCOME.

THE STUDENTS ARE VERY EXCITED FOR THIS, ROD!

WELL, I AM, TOO!

B-16

I ASSUMED THE STUDENTS WOULD BE *IN AWE* WITH A CELEBRITY INSTRUCTOR.

HOW WRONG I WAS.

MAY I ASK THE CAPTAIN, WHAT IS HIS PLEASURE? HOW MANY MUST DIE BEFORE HE IS SATISFIED?

OFFHAND, LIEUTENANT YAMURI, I WOULD SAY *ALL OF THEM.* I DON'T CARE WHERE THEY ARE, *WHO* THEY ARE-- IF THEY ARE THE *ENEMY* THEY ARE TO BE *DESTROYED.* FIRST DAY OF THE WAR, LAST DAY OF THE WAR, WE DESTROY THEM.

AS YOU CAN SEE, THE BINOCULARS ARE SIMPLY A *PLOT DEVICE.* BY PUTTING LIEUTENANT KATELL, LITERALLY, IN THE SHOES OF HIS ENEMY, WE CAN FORCE HIM INTO CHANGING HIS WORLD VIEW.

DON'T YOU THINK THE METAPHOR IS A LITTLE *ON THE NOSE?*

PLEASE ELABORATE.

WELL, THE PREMISE IS SOMEWHAT REDUCTIVE. THIS IS *OBVIOUSLY* YOUR STAB AT THE VIETNAM WAR. THE SITUATION THERE IS SO MULTIFACETED AND COMPLEX, AND YOU FLATTENED THE CHARACTERS INTO STEREOTYPES. IT'S *KINDER-GARTEN MORALITY.*

THE SHOW IS BROADCAST TO A WIDE AUDIENCE ALL ACROSS THE U.S.

CERTAIN COMPLEXITIES NEED TO BE IRONED OUT IN ORDER FOR THE AUDIENCE TO COMPREHEND THEM.

IF YOU SAY SO...

IN JANUARY OF 1964, I FINALLY GOT THE NOTICE.

THE TWILIGHT ZONE ENDED WITH A WHIMPER. AT THAT POINT, THE SHOW HAD FULLY RUN OUT OF STEAM.

WE THREW A LITTLE *"WAKE"* FOR THE SHOW, INVITING CAST AND CREW TO CELEBRATE A BITTERSWEET END.

TWILIGHT ZONE, CALIF
THIS PLACQUE
COMMEMORATES THE
128 PEOPLE KILLED
DURING THE COURSE OF
TURBULENT FIVE YEARS

TWILIGHT ZONE

R.I.P.

WELL, ROD, IT'S BEEN ONE HELL OF A RIDE.

YOU MEAN A *RIDE TO HELL?* IT'S HARD TO BELIEVE WE MADE IT OUT IN ONE PIECE.

ARE YOU SAD IT'S ALL OVER?

THERE'S A TOUCH OF SADNESS, SURE. BUT MOSTLY, I FEEL RELIEVED. LIKE A MASSIVE *BOULDER* HAS BEEN LIFTED OFF MY BACK.

SO, NOW THAT YOU'VE ESCAPED THE CLAWS OF *THE TWILIGHT ZONE,* WHAT'S NEXT?

YOU KNOW WHAT, RICH? I HAVEN'T THE *SLIGHTEST IDEA.*

IN THE FALL OF 1965, I SOLD MY REMAINING 50% SHARE IN *THE TWILIGHT ZONE* AHEAD OF THE SHOW'S SCHEDULED SYNDICATION.

I RECEIVED A SUM CLOSE TO HALF A MILLION DOLLARS FOR THE RIGHTS.

CBS HAD CONVINCED ME THAT THE SHOW WOULD NEVER RECOUP ITS LOSSES. THEY WERE DOING ME A *FAVOR.*

I WAS *SURE* MY DECISION WAS SOUND.

I WOULD LATER GREATLY REGRET THE SALE.

THE TWILIGHT ZONE WOULD SCORE OUTSTANDING RATINGS IN SYNDICATION, BECOMING *A CULT HIT.*

I WISH I'D HAD MORE *LASTING FAITH* IN MY OWN CREATION.

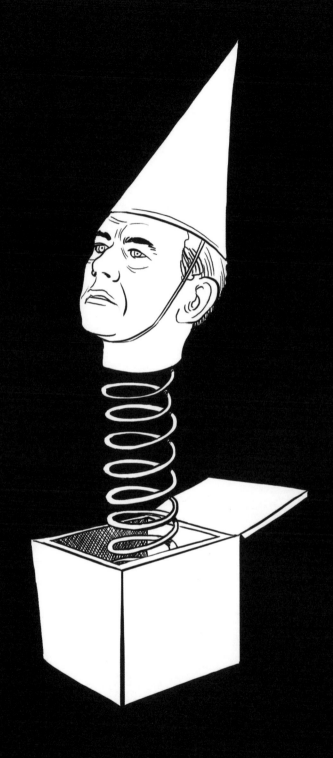

PART IV

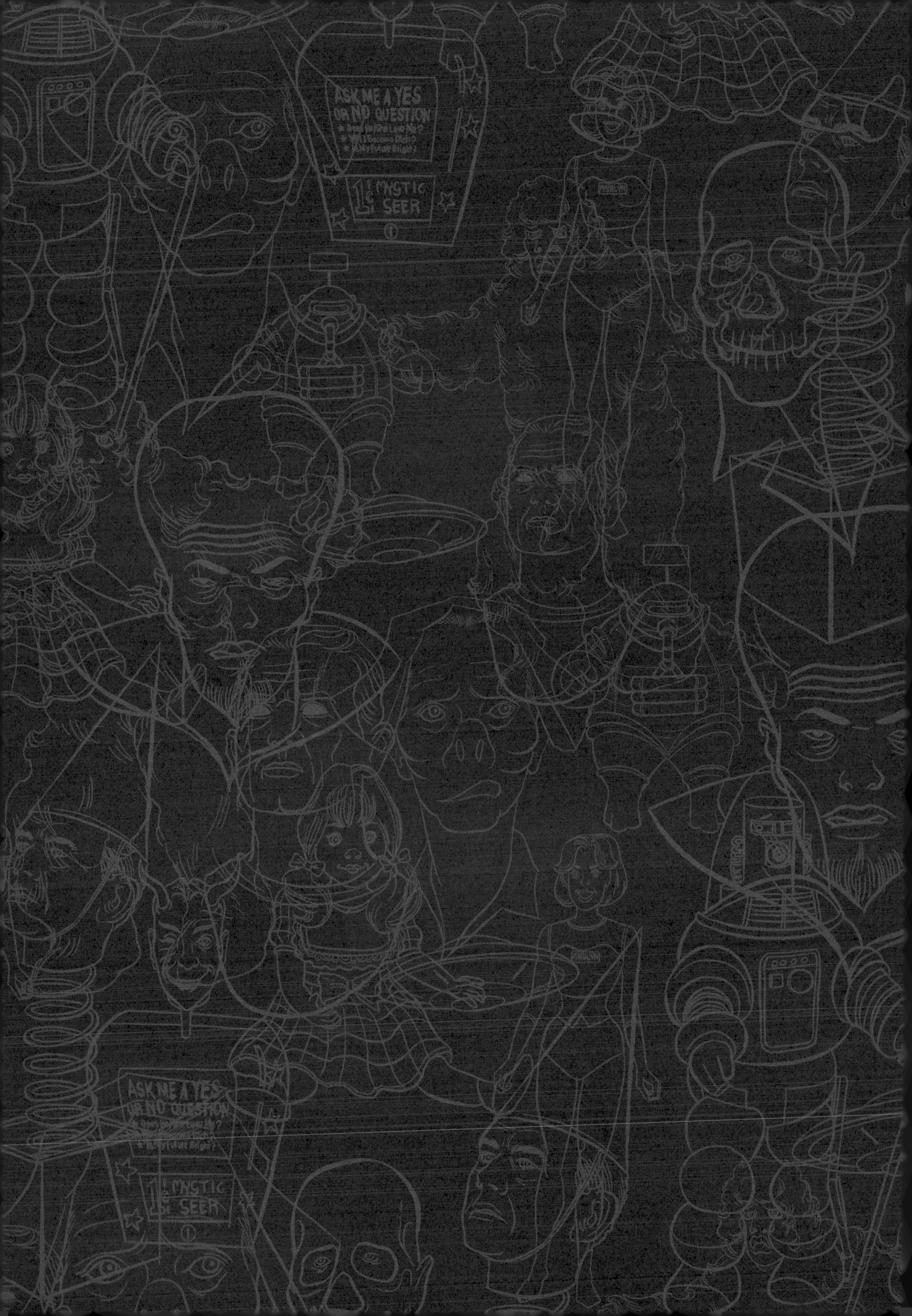
ASK ME A YES OR NO QUESTION
1¢ MYSTIC SEER
ASK ME A YES OR NO QUESTION
1¢ MYSTIC SEER

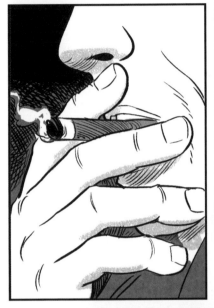

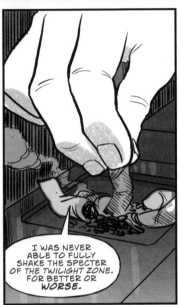

I WAS NEVER ABLE TO FULLY SHAKE THE SPECTER OF THE TWILIGHT ZONE. FOR BETTER OR **WORSE.**

COME NOW, WITH ALL YOUR CONNECTIONS AND MOMENTUM? YOU MUST HAVE HAD SOMETHING UP YOUR SLEEVE.

THERE WAS **SOMETHING** BREWING.

A SHOW I HAD PREVIOUSLY PITCHED WAS NOW PUT INTO GEAR.

THE LONER...

...IT WAS AN EXISTENTIAL WESTERN.

IT FEATURED A FORMER UNION CAVALRY WHO WAS AIMLESSLY DRIFTING IN THE VASTNESS OF THE NEW FRONTIER.

EACH EPISODE WOULD SHOWCASE A NEW ENCOUNTER ON HIS JOURNEY.

THAT SOUNDS LIKE A GOOD PREMISE.

I THOUGHT SO, TOO. I WANTED IT TO BE THOUGHT-PROVOKING. NO SCHLOCKY GUNPLAY, NO BANK ROBBERIES AND NONE OF THE HORSE CHASES YOU SAW IN ALL THE OTHER TV WESTERNS.

BUT CBS WANTED PRECISELY *THAT*. THE PILOT WAS TOO CEREBRAL. THE STRUGGLES TOO INTERNAL.

THEY TOLD ME I HAD TO PUT MORE *ACTION* IN THE SHOW-- MORE GUNPLAY AND HORSE CHASES.

I WAS SICK OF THE MEN IN GREY SUITS PUSHING ME AROUND. SO I TOOK MY GRIEVANCES TO THE PRESS--NAMING NAMES, CRITICIZING THE NETWORK'S LACK OF VISION.

A GUTSY MOVE. HOW DID THEY TAKE IT?

NOT WELL.

"THE ANGRY YOUNG MAN" HAD FINALLY CROSSED THE LINE.

THE SHOW, WHICH HAD ALSO SUFFERED FROM POOR RATINGS, WAS CANCELLED AFTER ONLY ONE SEASON.

AND I WAS *EXILED* FROM CBS FOREVER...THE NETWORK WHICH HAD BEEN MY *HOME* FOR SO MANY YEARS.

AS THE SIXTIES WERE DRAWING TO A CLOSE, MY FUTURE AS A WRITER LOOKED MORE UNCERTAIN THAN EVER. I BELIEVE THAT WAS THE MOMENT I REALLY STARTED TO STRAY FROM MY PATH.

A PICNIC WAS SUPPOSED TO HAPPEN HERE.

IT WASN'T RAINED OUT. *BUGGED OUT.* BY MOSQUITOS, FLIES, GNATS.

A PICNIC COULD HAVE HAPPENED HERE, WITH *6-12 PLUS.*

THE PLUS IS A FORMULA WITH *TWO* ACTIVE INGREDIENTS, *NOT ONE.*

MADE SPECIALLY TO PROTECT *REAL* OUTDOOR PEOPLE.

MAN OVER MOSQUITO. 6-12 PLUS: THE INSECT REPELLANT FOR REAL OUTDOOR PEOPLE.

CUT! FANTASTIC WORK EVERYONE. IT'S A WRAP.

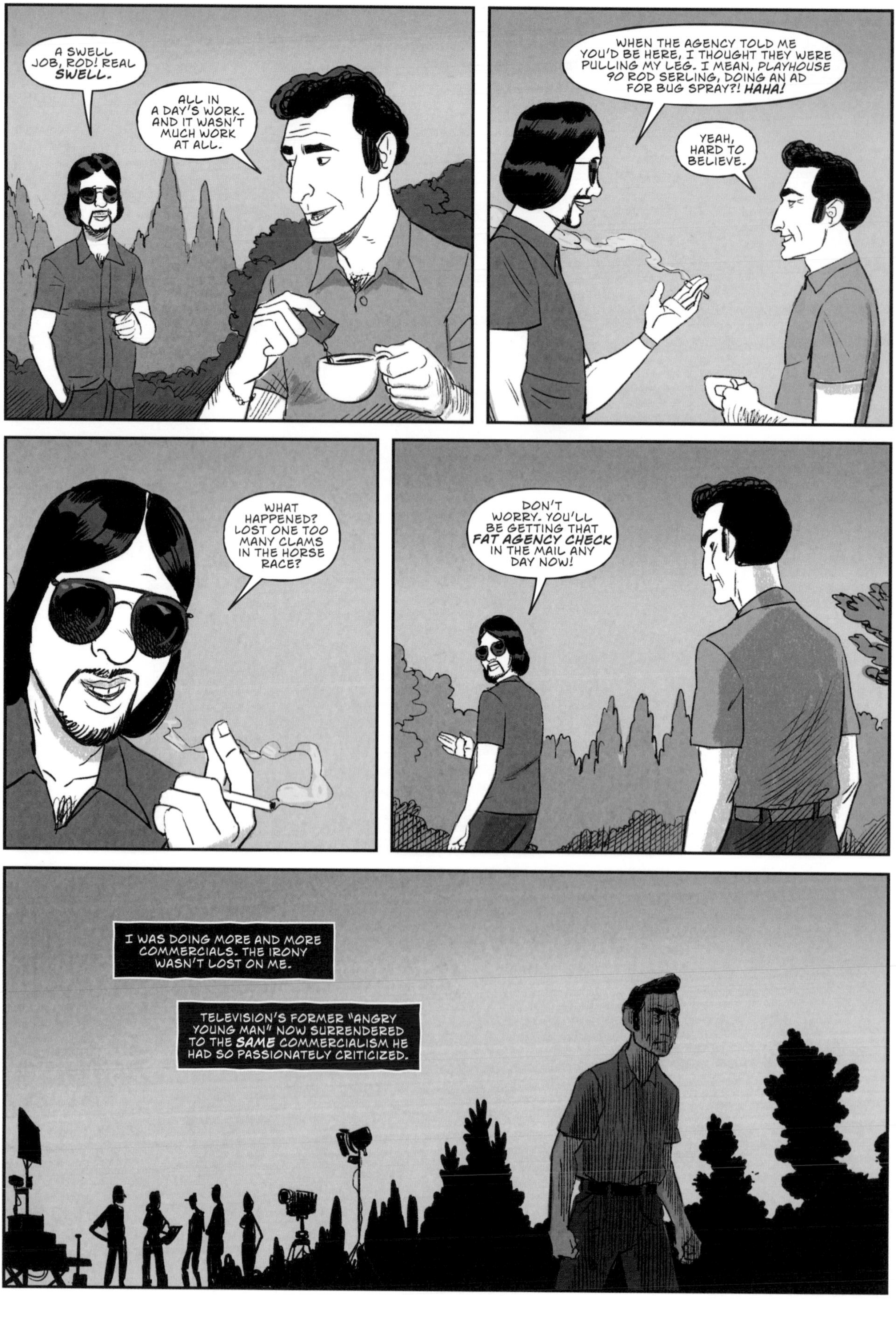
A SWELL JOB, ROD! REAL SWELL.
ALL IN A DAY'S WORK. AND IT WASN'T MUCH WORK AT ALL.
WHEN THE AGENCY TOLD ME YOU'D BE HERE, I THOUGHT THEY WERE PULLING MY LEG. I MEAN, PLAYHOUSE 90 ROD SERLING, DOING AN AD FOR BUG SPRAY?! HAHA!
YEAH, HARD TO BELIEVE.
WHAT HAPPENED? LOST ONE TOO MANY CLAMS IN THE HORSE RACE?
DON'T WORRY. YOU'LL BE GETTING THAT FAT AGENCY CHECK IN THE MAIL ANY DAY NOW!
I WAS DOING MORE AND MORE COMMERCIALS. THE IRONY WASN'T LOST ON ME.
TELEVISION'S FORMER "ANGRY YOUNG MAN" NOW SURRENDERED TO THE SAME COMMERCIALISM HE HAD SO PASSIONATELY CRITICIZED.

I WAS LOOKING FOR REASSURANCE IN ALL SORTS OF ODD PLACES.

I JUST CAN'T BELIEVE I'M SITTING HERE AND TALKING WITH YOU! YOU'RE GOING TO TURN INTO A WEREWOLF ANY MINUTE, AREN'T YOU?

IT'S NOT A FULL MOON, CINDY, SO I ASSURE YOU, THERE'S NOTHING TO WORRY ABOUT.

OHH! THAT ONE EPISODE WITH *THE DOLL* GAVE ME SUCH *CHILLS!*

I COULDN'T SLEEP FOR *A WEEK* AFTER.

I'M SORRY TO HEAR THAT.

NO, NO! IT WAS *GROOVY.* LIKE A GOOD KIND OF SCARE. GETS YOU ALL *TINGLY.*

SO WHAT ISSUE OF THE MAGAZINE WERE YOU IN?

SEPTEMBER, BUT I WASN'T A CENTERFOLD. THEY JUST FEATURED ME IN A SPECIAL "SPACE AGE" PHOTO SHOOT.

I WORE A SILVER SPACE HELMET, HAD A LASER GUN...AND WELL...THAT'S ABOUT IT.

I BELIEVE I REMEMBER THOSE PICTURES.

YOU DO, DO YOU?

LATER.

WHERE ARE WE GOING?

OVER HERE.

SEE, I'VE GOT SOME MAGIC TRICKS UP MY SLEEVE.

YOU'RE A MASTER OF THE ARCANE ARTS?

I WISH. HEF JUST GAVE ME THE KEY...

I WAS TRYING TO MAKE A CAREER FOR MYSELF AS A FEATURE FILM WRITER. BUT IT WASN'T EASY. AT THE TIME, I WAS STRUGGLING WITH A SCREENPLAY FOR KING BROTHERS PRODUCTIONS.

WHILE I WAS WRITING AND REWRITING, THE FILM RIGHTS CHANGED HANDS AND PRODUCER ARTHUR P. JACOBS TOOK THE HELM.

PLANET OF THE APES
Pierre Boulle
AUTHOR OF THE BRIDGE OVER THE RIVER KWAI

MY EARLIEST VERSION OF THE SCREENPLAY FEATURED AN APE CITY-- A MODERN METROPOLIS WITH HIGHRISES, CARS, TRAINS...

BUT ONCE THE PRODUCERS READ IT, IT BECAME CLEAR THAT A CITY OF THAT SCOPE WOULD BE TOO COSTLY.

YOU'LL HAVE TO FIND SOME WORK-AROUND. WE DON'T HAVE THAT KIND OF BUDGET.

SO I REWROTE THE SCRIPT WITH AN EYE FOR A VERY DIFFERENT SOCIETY, ONE THAT WAS IN LIMBO--A SEMI-PRIMITIVE CIVILIZATION.

I ADDED ONE OF MY TRADEMARK **TWIST ENDINGS**, WHICH DIFFERED COMPLETELY FROM THE ORIGINAL BOOK.

CORNELIUS: MR. THOMAS, RUN! PLEASE! FOR GOD'S SAKE, *RUN!*

THOMAS: I'M AFRAID... I'M AFRAID THERE'S NO PLACE TO RUN *TO*...

I'M AFRAID THERE'S NO PLACE TO GO... NOW.

AFTER I SUBMITTED MY FINAL DRAFT IN '65, THE FORMERLY BLACKLISTED SCREENWRITER MICHAEL WILSON WAS HIRED TO REWRITE THE SCRIPT.

WILSON REVISED THE DIALOGUE, MADE THE STORY MORE HUMOROUS AND LESS SOMBER, AND, OF COURSE, ADDED MANY ACTION SCENES.

THIS WAS A REAL BLOW. BUT I WAS PROMISED CO-CREDIT FOR THE FILM AND REMAINED ON GOOD TERMS WITH THE PRODUCTION.

I LIKE YOUR GET-UP, CHARLTON.

I BELIEVE THIS "OUTFIT" WAS IN YOUR SCRIPT, PAL!

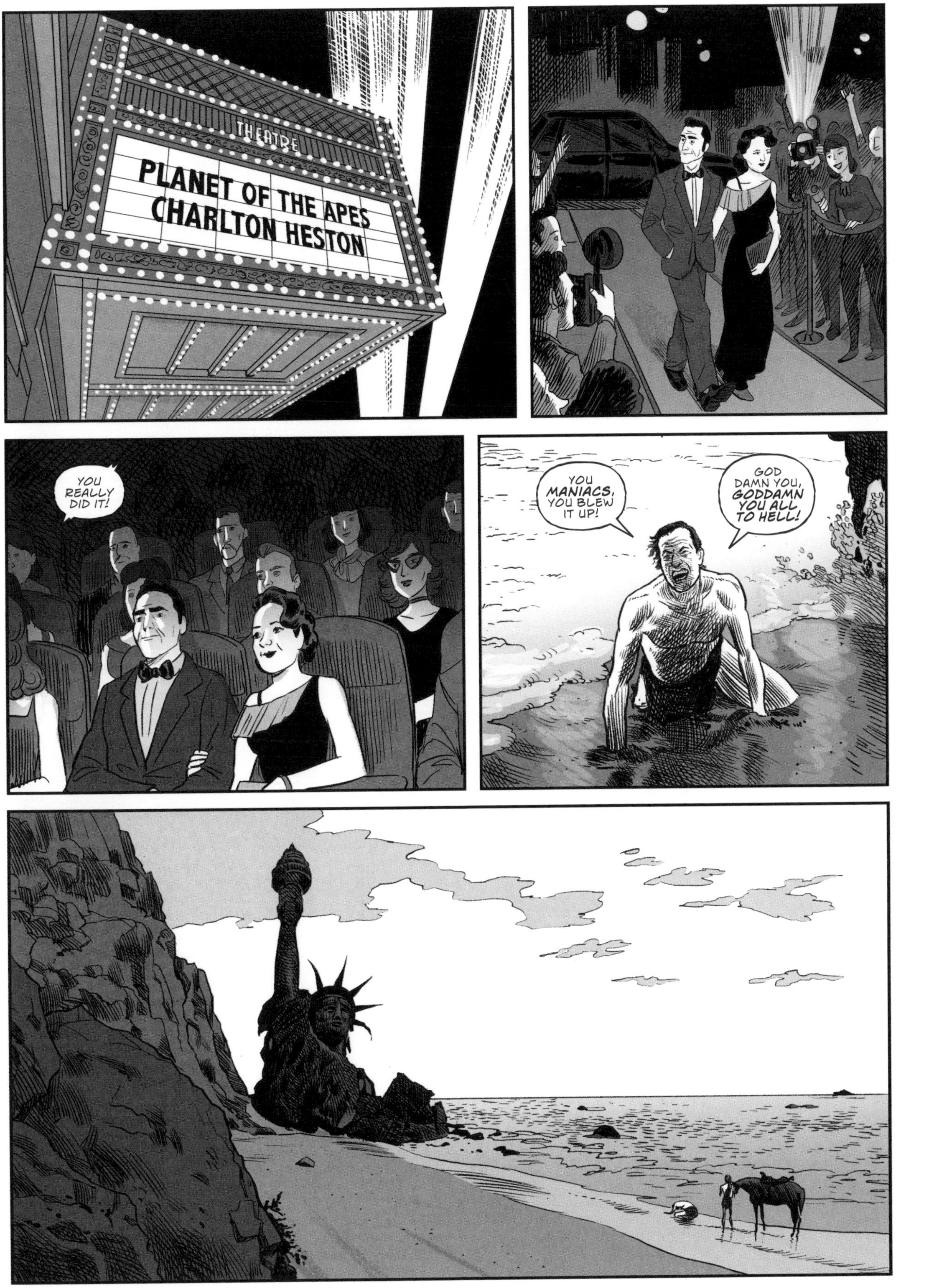
THEATRE
PLANET OF THE APES
CHARLTON HESTON
YOU REALLY DID IT!
YOU MANIACS, YOU BLEW IT UP!
GOD DAMN YOU, GODDAMN YOU ALL TO HELL!

WELCOME TO TODAY'S MEETING OF *THE LIAR'S CLUB.* IF YOU DON'T KNOW WHAT THIS OBJECT IS, OR WHAT IT'S USED FOR, THEN SETTLE BACK! THE TALL TALES ARE ABOUT TO BEGIN!

FIRST, WE'D LIKE YOU TO WELCOME ONE OF AMERICA'S GREAT STORYTELLERS, AND PRESIDENT OF THE LIAR'S CLUB, ROD SERLING!

THANK YOU VERY MUCH! LADIES AND GENTLEMEN, I'M NIKITA KHRUSHCHEV, AND OVER HERE ARE THREE MEMBERS OF THE KREMLIN RIDING A TRICYCLE.

WE'RE ALL LIARS HERE!

NOW, WE MEET OUR CONTESTANTS. THEY ARE: JUDY SANSORINO, A HOUSEWIFE FROM BURBANK...

AND HER OPPONENT, MR. TOM PAIGE, A STUDENT FROM VAN NUYS.

NOW, OUR PANEL OF LIARS KNOWS THE EXACT DESCRIPTION OF EACH OF OUR OBJECTS. BUT THEY ARE GOING TO TELL YOU DIFFERENT STORIES ABOUT THEM. THE PLAYER THAT RECOGNIZES THE *TRUTH* THE MOST NUMBER OF TIMES WILL RECEIVE ONE HUNDRED DOLLARS!

THE OFFERS WERE NOT POURING IN ANYMORE, AND I TOOK WHAT CAME MY WAY. GOD KNOWS THERE WAS NO GOOD REASON FOR ME TO HOST *THE LIAR'S CLUB.* THE PAY WAS PALTRY.

PERHAPS I JUST ENJOYED BEING ON CAMERA ONCE AGAIN.

IN LATE 1968, *NIGHT GALLERY* WAS GREENLIT--A MADE-FOR-TELEVISION MOVIE PRODUCED BY UNIVERSAL AND CREATED BY ME.

AS THE SHOOT APPROACHED, WE BEGAN TO HIT SOME SNAGS.

RING RING

HELLO?

WHO IS IT?

IT'S *JOAN CRAWFORD.*

DOESN'T SHE KNOW WHAT *TIME* IT IS?? I WISH YOU HAD NEVER GIVEN HER OUR HOME PHONE!

YES, JOAN. WHAT IS IT?

I'M TERRIBLY SORRY TO CALL YOU AT THIS ODD HOUR OF THE NIGHT, BUT I'M *TREMENDOUSLY* NERVOUS. I'VE NOT BEEN ABLE TO SLEEP FOR DAYS NOW.

WHAT SEEMS TO BE THE PROBLEM?

IT'S JUST-- WELL, I CAN'T *BELIEVE* UNIVERSAL WOULD LET A TWENTY-YEAR-OLD *CHILD* DIRECT A MADE-FOR-TELEVISION MOVIE. THAT'S SIMPLY *UNHEARD OF!*

I'M SURE THE KID'S *HIGHLY CAPABLE* IF THEY TRUST HIM TO DIRECT.

CAPABLE? MY CAREER'S ON THE LINE HERE, ROD! I CAN'T LET A CHILD DIRECT ME. THIS COULD END UP BEING A MAJOR *DISASTER!*

LISTEN, JOAN. *TRUST ME,* THIS KID-- WHAT WAS HIS NAME...? SPIELBERG!--WILL DO A FABULOUS JOB! WE HAVE A GREAT STORY FOR YOU. HOW ABOUT WE TALK TOMORROW AFTERNOON?

≒GRUMBLE≒

THE *NIGHT GALLERY* MADE-FOR-TELEVISION MOVIE RAN ON NBC THE NIGHT OF NOVEMBER 8TH, 1969.

GOOD EVENING, AND WELCOME TO A PRIVATE SHOWING OF *THREE PAINTINGS*, DISPLAYED HERE FOR THE FIRST TIME.

EACH IS A COLLECTOR'S ITEM IN ITS OWN WAY. NOT BECAUSE OF ANY SPECIAL ARTISTIC QUALITY, BUT BECAUSE EACH CAPTURES ON A CANVAS—SUSPENDS IN TIME AND SPACE—A FROZEN MOMENT...OF A *NIGHTMARE.*

I WANT TO *SEE* SOMETHING! TREES, CONCRETE, BUILDINGS, GRASS, AIRPLANES!

COLOR!

THANK YOU, *THANK YOU!*

NO! NO!

THE *NIGHT GALLERY* MOVIE GOT OUTSTANDING RATINGS. BUT IN SPITE OF THAT, NBC WAS RELUCTANT TO TURN IT INTO AN ONGOING SHOW.

ANTHOLOGY SHOWS WERE A THING OF THE *PAST*, OR SO THEY THOUGHT.

THE OLD FIGHTER IN ME WOULDN'T GIVE UP SO EASILY. I PRESSURED MY AGENTS, AND I PULLED EVERY TRICK I HAD LEFT UP MY SLEEVE.

HAVE THEY READ MY LAST LETTER?

YOU HAVE TO KEEP *PUSHING* THEM--

YES, I *KNOW* YOU TALKED TO UNIVERSAL EARLIER THIS WEEK. CALL *AGAIN!*

YOUR AGENT'S ON THE LINE! HE SAID THERE'S *GOOD NEWS!*

HAROLD? WHAT'S GOING ON?

UNIVERSAL SAID "YES." AND NBC'S ON BOARD AS WELL.

YES! YOU'VE MADE MY DAY!

BEFORE YOU CELEBRATE, ROD, THERE'S SOME *DETAILS* YOU NEED TO KNOW.

LAY IT ON ME.

YOU'LL BE HOSTING, AND NARRATING. THEY WILL PRODUCE ONLY SIX HOUR-LONG EPISODES TO START. THEY WANT YOU TO WRITE SOME OF THE SCRIPTS, BUT NOT *ALL*.

THEY'RE BEING CAUTIOUS, THAT'S TO BE EXPECTED.

HERE'S THE RINGER THOUGH: YOU HAVE *NO* CREATIVE CONTROL OVER THE SERIES.

UNIVERSAL WANTS THEIR *OWN* MAN IN CHARGE, A PRODUCER NAMED *JACK LAIRD*.

THE STUDIO KNEW HOW *DESPERATE* I WAS. WITHOUT MUCH HESITATION, I AGREED TO THEIR TERMS. EXCITED BY THE PROSPECT OF THE SHOW.

WELL, MAYBE WE CAN RENEGOTIATE LATER ON...

UNIVERSAL STUDIOS

THE SHOW BEGAN PRODUCTION SOON AFTER.

CUT!

THAT'S IT FOR TODAY, THANK YOU, ROD!

HEY JACK, I WAS WONDERING IF YOU HAD A CHANCE TO LOOK OVER THE SCRIPT I SENT YOU THE OTHER DAY.

TAKE IT EASY, ROD, YOU'RE THE *TALENT* TODAY. I'LL READ YOUR SCRIPT SOON, I *PROMISE.*

Jack Laird

MR. LAIRD, IT'S *ROD SERLING* ON THE PHONE.

TELL HIM I'M NOT HERE.

SO HAVE YOU TWO *NINCOMPOOPS* FINISHED READING THE SCRIPTS?

WHICH ONES DID YOU THINK MIGHT WORK?

WELL, THIS ONE *ROD* WROTE IS PRETTY GOOD.

AH YES, YES. I READ THAT ONE. NOT BAD, BUT TOO MORBID. *TYPICAL SERLING*. LET'S CHANGE THE ENDING. I WANT SOMETHING MORE *UPBEAT*.

SHOULD WE NOTIFY ROD?

NOTIFY HIM? WHY WOULD WE DO THAT?

AS THE PRODUCTION PROGRESSED, MY SCRIPTS WERE EITHER COMPLETELY RE-WRITTEN OR IGNORED. HOW NAIVE I WAS TO GIVE UP CREATIVE CONTROL SO EASILY.

TO SAY I WAS DISAPPOINTED WITH *NIGHT GALLERY* WOULD BE AN UNDERSTATEMENT. EXCLUDING A FEW GOOD MOMENTS, IT LOOKED, AT TIMES, LIKE A *PARODY* OF THE *TWILIGHT ZONE*.

I FOUND MYSELF SPENDING MORE AND MORE TIME AT MY LAKE HOUSE IN ITHACA.

LOOK AT DAVID, DAD!

GROOVY! I DIG HIS NEW LOOK!

YOU KNOW, I REALIZE *NOW* THAT THIS IS WHAT I'VE NEEDED ALL ALONG.

WHAT DO YOU MEAN?

HOLLYWOOD... IT'S BECOMING TOO *PAINFUL.*

TINSELTOWN IS TAKING ME APART ONE PIECE AT A TIME.

BUT EVERY TIME I'M BACK HERE, I FEEL LIKE I'M *HEALING*. SLOWLY PUTTING THE PIECES BACK TOGETHER.

THEN YOU SHOULD SPEND MORE TIME HERE.

THAT'S THE PLAN.

EVERYTHING OKAY, HONEY?

YES. YES. IT'S ALL GOOD.

EVERYTHING'S FINE.

I WAS ENJOYING TEACHING NOW MORE THAN EVER. AND THE STUDENTS WERE ALSO TREATING ME WITH A HIGHER LEVEL OF *RESPECT*.

PERHAPS I'D COME INTO MY *OWN* AS AN INSTRUCTOR.

BUT WHAT MADE YOU CHOOSE THE *BOXER* AS YOUR VEHICLE FOR THE STORY?

THERE'S SOMETHING INHERENTLY *TRAGIC* IN THE SPORT OF BOXING. HARLAN "MOUNTAIN" McCLINTOCK IS NOT A VICTIM OF HIS OWN CHOICES, BUT A VICTIM OF THE *SYSTEM*.

THE MOMENT HE'S UNABLE TO *WIN*, UNABLE TO ENTERTAIN, HE IS EJECTED INTO A COLD WORLD THAT DOESN'T *NEED* HIM.

COULDN'T HE *REINVENT* HIMSELF? FIND A NEW VOCATION?

THERE COMES A TIME WHEN A MAN HAS GIVEN *SO* MUCH OF HIMSELF TO HIS CHOSEN ENTERPRISE--

--THAT THERE'S *NOTHING* LEFT WITHIN HIM. HE LACKS THE DRIVE AND THE CONSTITUTION NECESSARY TO START ANEW.

ON A BRISK MAY MORNING IN 1975, I GOT UP EARLY, DETERMINED TO PREPARE THE SOIL FOR THE CORN I WAS PLANNING TO GROW.

≶HUFF, HUFF!≷

OOF! THIS THING'S HEAVY!

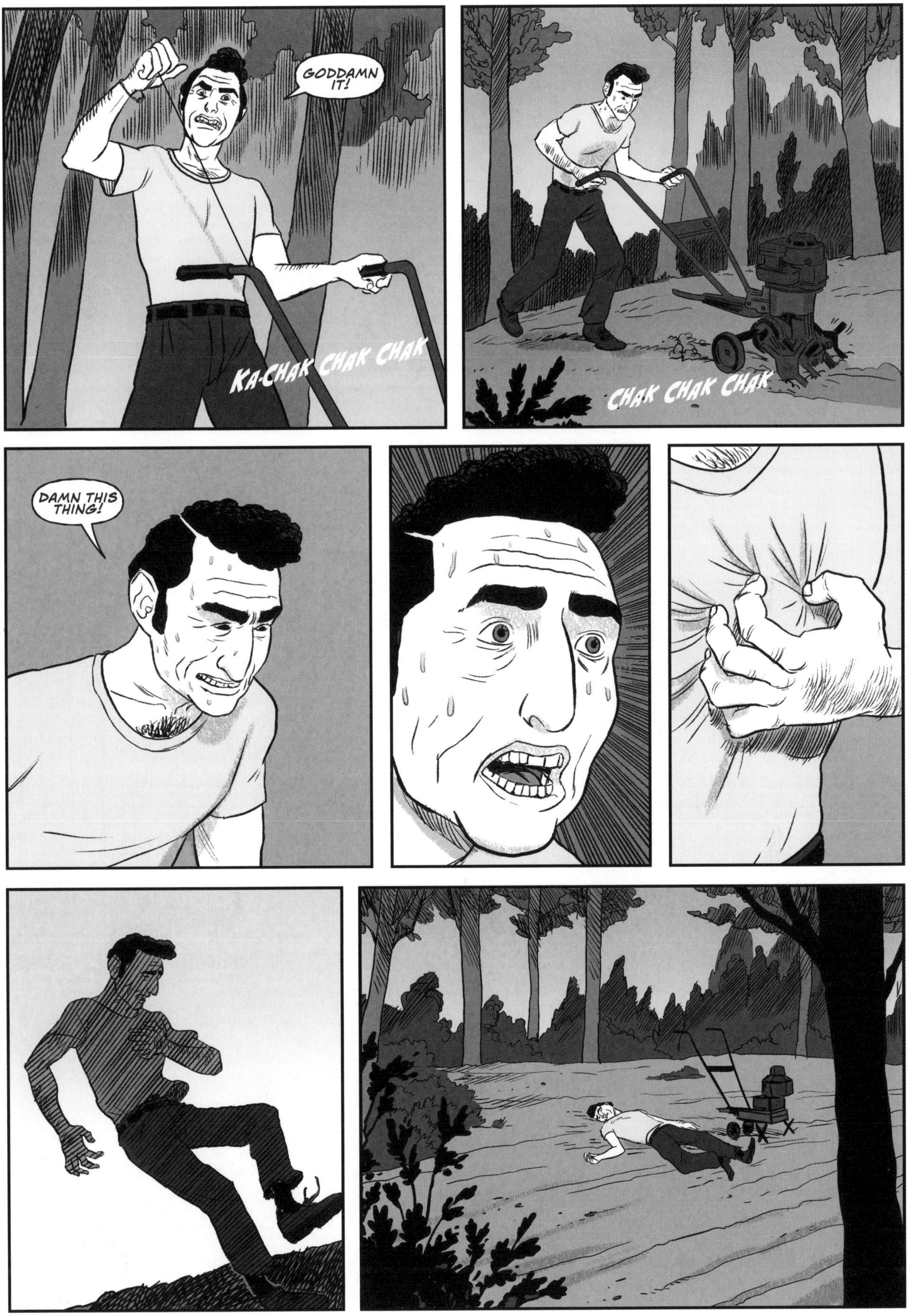
GODDAMN IT!
KA-CHAK CHAK CHAK
CHAK CHAK CHAK
DAMN THIS THING!

I WAS IN CARDIAC ARREST, AND RUSHED TO THE HOSPITAL...

I WAS WATCHING TV LAST NIGHT AND ALL OF A SUDDEN I HEAR YOUR VOICE, THEY HAD "THE HITCH-HIKER" ON!

HA! THAT'S A GOOD ONE!

IT'S NOT LOOKING GOOD.

A SECOND, MORE SEVERE HEART ATTACK CAME SEVERAL WEEKS LATER.

THE DOCTORS OPTED FOR OPEN HEART SURGERY, A RELATIVELY NEW, RISKY PROCEDURE.

ON JUNE 26TH, I WAS PUT UNDER ANESTHESIA AND ROLLED INTO THE OPERATING ROOM.

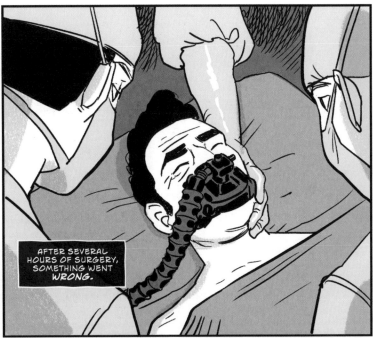

AFTER SEVERAL HOURS OF SURGERY, SOMETHING WENT **WRONG.**

BEEP...BEEP...BEEP...

BEEP...BEEP...

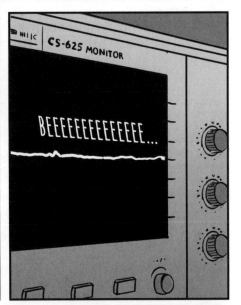

CS-625 MONITOR

BEEEEEEEEEEEEEE...

AFTER FIFTY YEARS ON THIS EARTH, I HAD REACHED THE **END OF THE ROAD.**

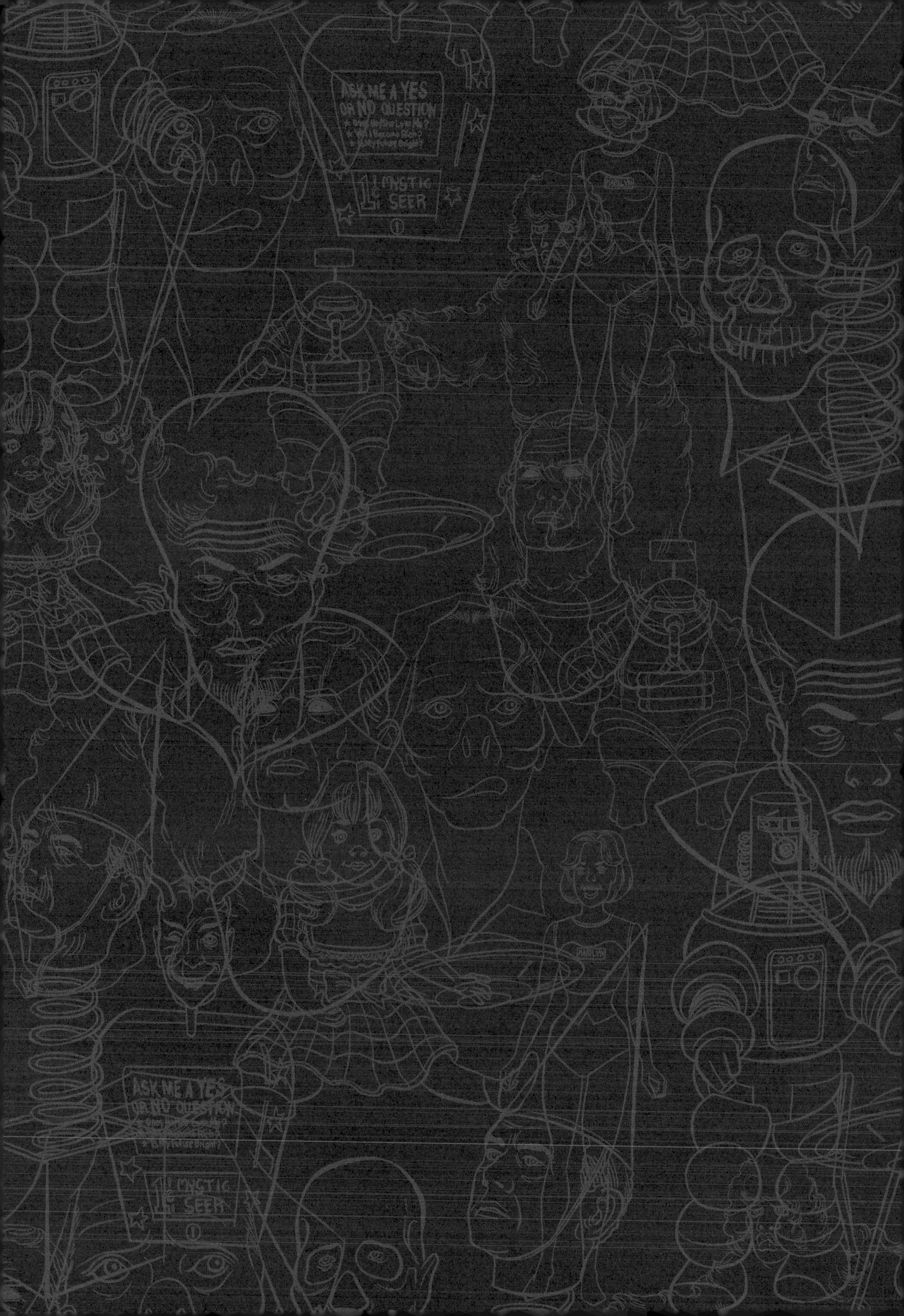
ASK ME A YES OR NO QUESTION
MYSTIC SEER
MARILYN

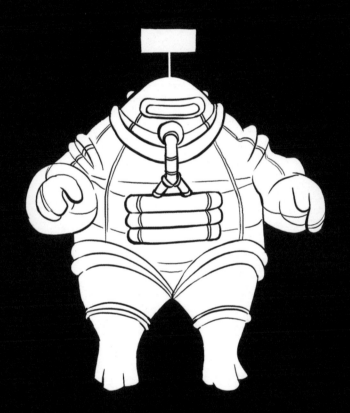

EPILOGUE

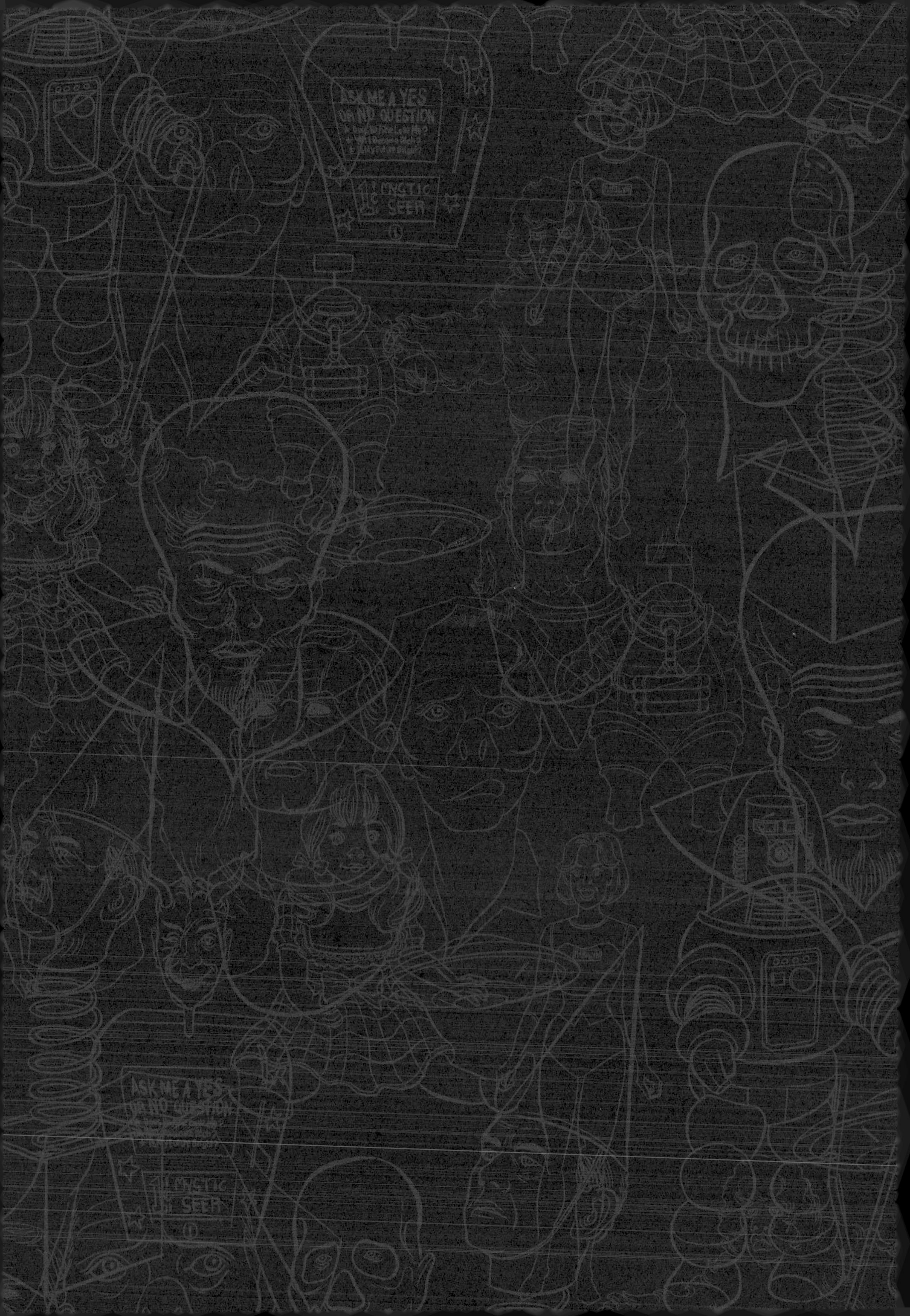
ASK ME A YES
OR NO QUESTION
MYSTIC
SEER

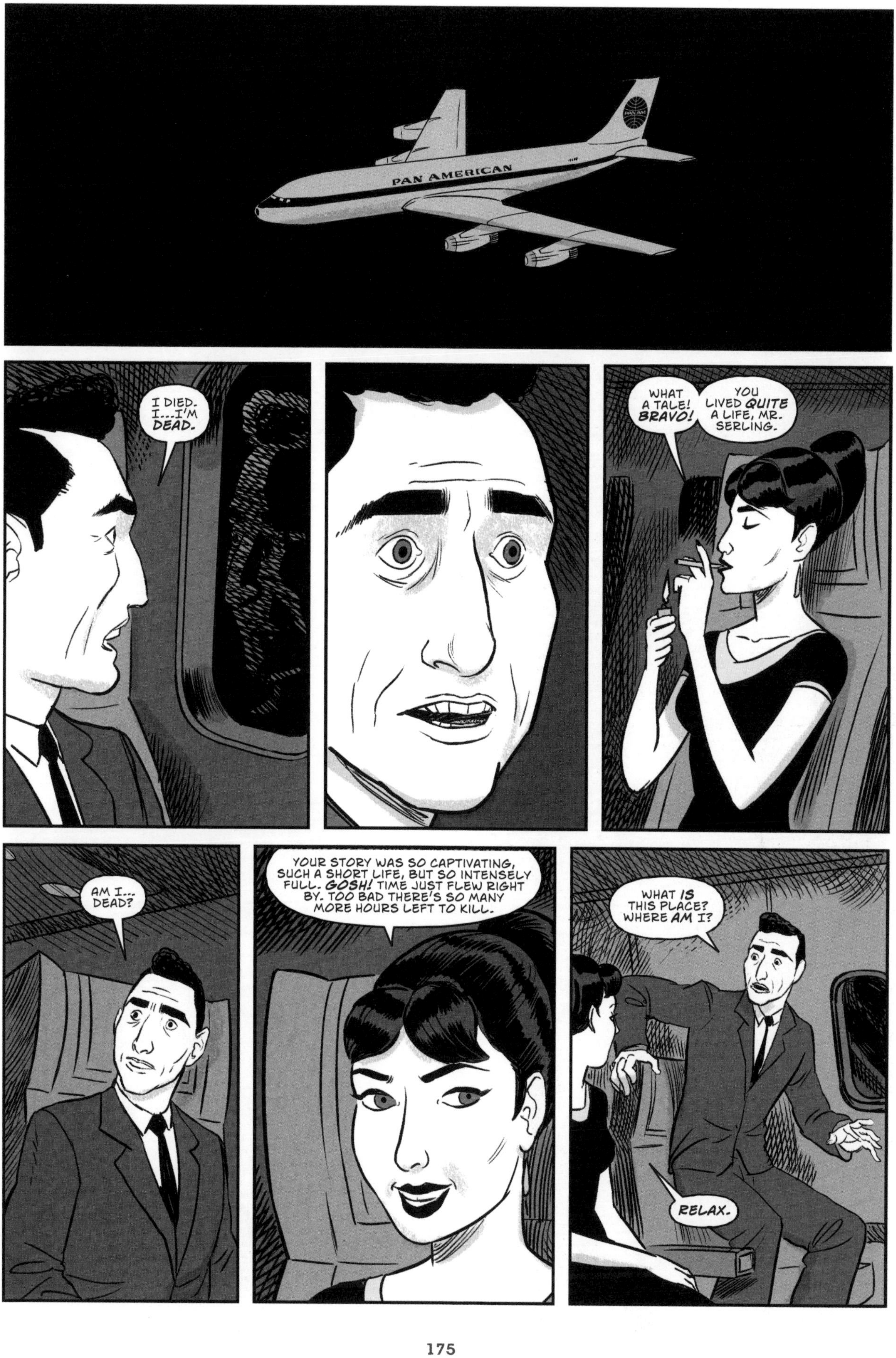
PAN AMERICAN
I DIED. I...I'M DEAD.
WHAT A TALE! BRAVO!
YOU LIVED QUITE A LIFE, MR. SERLING.
AM I... DEAD?
YOUR STORY WAS SO CAPTIVATING, SUCH A SHORT LIFE, BUT SO INTENSELY FULL. GOSH! TIME JUST FLEW RIGHT BY. TOO BAD THERE'S SO MANY MORE HOURS LEFT TO KILL.
WHAT IS THIS PLACE? WHERE AM I?
RELAX.

IT'S *QUITE* ALRIGHT, MR. SERLING.

YOU DON'T NEED TO WORRY. WE'RE TAKING YOU WHERE YOU NEED TO GO.

REST ASSURED, YOU WILL ARRIVE AT YOUR DESTINATION ...

...EVENTUALLY.

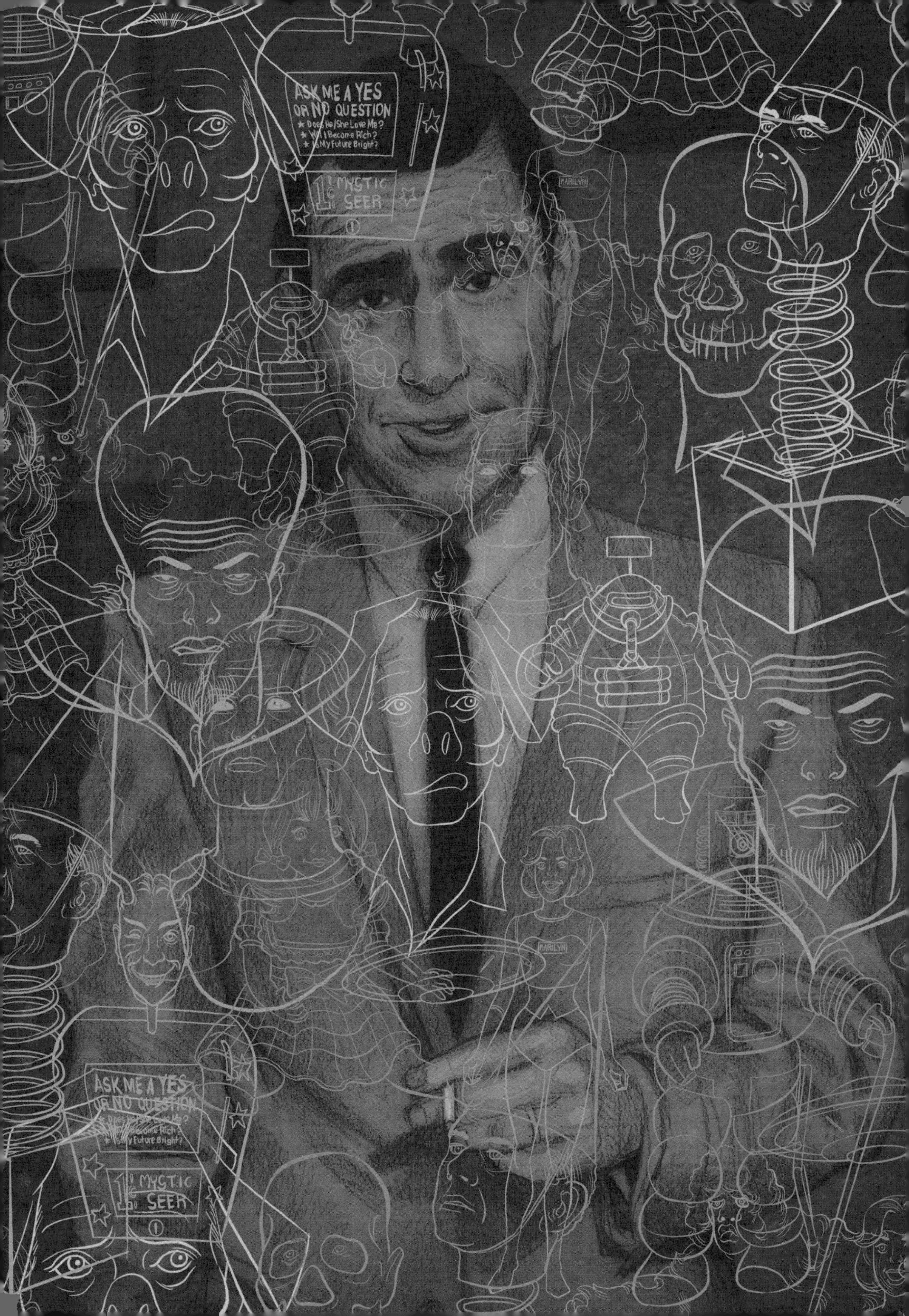
ASK ME A YES OR NO QUESTION
★ Does He/She Love Me?
★ Will I Become Rich?
★ Is My Future Bright?
1¢ MYSTIC SEER
MARILYN
ASK ME A YES
MYSTIC SEER
MARILYN

Beyond the Zone

I was a late visitor to the fifth dimension. Growing up in Israel in the 80s, there was a limited selection of old American shows that made the trans-Atlantic leap to our television screens. As far as classic shows went (the ones the network probably got on discount), there was only room for crowd-pleasers such as *I Love Lucy* and *Happy Days*. We were lucky enough to have the original *Star Trek*, but sadly, *The Twilight Zone* never made the cut.

The first time I was exposed to the show (indirectly) was through its 1985 reboot, which *did* make it to Israel. I remember a few episodes being interesting, but nothing left a lasting impression. Throughout my teens, I would encounter references to *The Twilight Zone* in popular culture. *The Simpsons*, *The Wonder Years* and many others would pay tribute to the show. These allusions were lost on me. Even after I moved to the U.S., it would be years before I was exposed to the original broadcast.

I wish I had a more exciting story of how I eventually got to see the *The Twilight Zone*. Like, maybe I'd found an abandoned DVD collection on a stoop, or saw "To Serve Man" screened on a wall at a Halloween party. In reality, I finally watched the show in 2009, when it became available on Netflix. I thought I'd see what all the fuss was about. Next thing I knew, I was being swallowed whole by a black and white vortex of strangeness.

Some episodes were so perfect I could not believe they actually ran on television—and in the 1950s and early '60s at that! They were beautiful, gray-toned gems with eye-popping visuals and stranger-than-strange stories. I consumed all five seasons of the show within a few weeks, rationing the episodes like a man starving away in a cave. One thing that struck me about *The Twilight Zone* was how gloomy it was; at times, the episodes felt like they had more in common with the films of Ingmar Bergman than with any television series. They dealt with heavy stuff—mortality, identity, the nature of man. Serling may have converted to Unitarianism, but his creations felt Jewish in nature. To me, they echo the old Jewish *Mashals* and *Maasiyas* (Fables and Tales).

And who was this man in the gray suit? Smoking like there was no tomorrow, his voice tightly wound like a tripwire? A deep sense of existential anxiety runs at the core of *The Twilight Zone*, and it conveys some deep truth about its creator. Serling was, after all, a product of World War II—a war that was perhaps the greatest traumatic event in the history of humanity. And the trauma echoes within many of Serling's creations. After the war, America rose to the status of a world superpower. It was a daydream of gleaming chrome, bright white smiles, and bleach-blond hair. But behind the perfect veneer lay something else completely—strange monsters, quivering with fear and anger. Serling was able to see those monsters, walking in broad daylight—then capture and pin them down on paper.

After I finished the show, I was so inspired I created an illustration of the enigmatic host. As I was drawing the clenched smile, I thought to myself, maybe Serling would be a good subject for a graphic novel? I needed to find out more. So I ordered a few biographies and told myself I would

The road to the perfect cover: Koren offered many sketch options for the cover as evidenced here.

give them a good read very soon—maybe there was something there that could be turned into a comic.

Somehow, the books ended up on the top shelf of my bookcase. They sat there, collecting dust, year after year, while I worked on different projects. Finally, in 2016, I was once again on the lookout for my next undertaking. I glanced up at the top shelf of my bookcase, and there they sat, waiting. I blew the dust off and began to read.

As I was writing the script for the book, the world around me seemed to become more and more like the Twilight Zone. Donald Trump was elected president. White Supremacists were coming out of the woodworks. California was set ablaze and a variety of other natural disasters were striking the U.S. Paul Krugman of *The New York Times* wrote an Op-Ed titled "Living in The Trump Zone," where he compared the new president to Anthony Fremont, the godlike monster-child from the classic episode "It's a Good Life."

Again and again, *The Twilight Zone* was mentioned in the news. It all made perfect sense to me. After all, Serling had grown up in a world that had gone completely nuts. He had lived through war and seen senseless death and killing firsthand. He had returned to an all-powerful America, a country on the rise, yet in a state of deep terror of the atomic bomb. Anxiety and uncertainty were in the air, and Serling was able to channel them, perhaps better than anyone, in the then-modest and still formless medium of television. Now, once again, anxiety was thick in the air.

During the process of researching the book, I was exposed to Serling's other great works, such as "Patterns," "The Velvet Alley" and "Requiem for a Heavyweight." Serling had his heart in the right place, and wrote scripts with a deep sense of humanism on such subjects as the corrosive nature of success, the oppression of the individual by large systems, and the deep flaws built into human society.

So here I am, three years later, and I feel like I have to say goodbye to a friend. I take down some reference shots of Serling from my studio wall, and suddenly I feel sad. I didn't know him; in fact, he died before I was even born, but there was something about his work that struck a chord with me. After putting the photos away, I decide to go to a local coffee shop to finish up this essay. After writing for a while, I take a break from the glare of my laptop screen and look up. Serling's ubiquitous face stares right back at me. I realize the corner I sit in is the Jacques Cousteau corner, adorned with old records, books and other paraphernalia. Serling's face is printed on the back of an old laser disc titled "The Undersea World of Jacques Cousteau," which he narrated.

Is this a sign? Is Serling trying to tell me something from beyond the grave? In any case, it's time for me to say a final goodbye to the friend I never knew.

– Koren Shadmi

Bibliography

Adams, Val. "'Twilight Zone' to expand in '63: Rod Serling Will Produce 13 Hour-Long C.B.S. Dramas." *New York Times*, May 24, 1962.

Andrews, Ralph. *Liar's Club*. Hosted by Rod Serling. 1969; Various Networks, 1969–1970. TV Program.

Barnouw, Erik. *The Golden Web: A History of Broadcasting in the United States, Volume 2: 1933 to 1953*. New York: Oxford University Press, 1968.

Barnouw, Erik. *The Image Empire: A History of Broadcasting in the United States, Vol. 3: From 1953*. New York: Oxford University Press, 1970.

Brevelle, Linda. "Rod Serling: The Facts of Life (Rod Serling's Final Interview)." *Writer's Digest Magazine*, 1976.

Cook, Fielder, dir. *Kraft Television Theatre*. Season 8, Episode 20, "Patterns." Written by Rod Serling. Aired January 12, 1955, on NBC.

Cook, Fielder, dir. *Playhouse 90*. Season 4, Episode 17, "In the Presence of Mine Enemies." Written by Rod Serling. Aired May 18, 1960, on CBS.

Corman, Roger, dir. *The House of Usher*. Written by Edgar Allen Poe and Richard Matheson. 1960; Japan: MGM, 1960. Film.

Eller, Jonathan R. *Ray Bradbury Unbound*. Illinois: University of Illinois Press, 2014.

Engel, Joel. *Rod Serling: The Dreams and Nightmares of Life in the Twilight Zone*. Chicago: Contemporary Books, 1989.

Frankenheimer, John, dir. *Playhouse 90*. Season 3, Episode 2, "Days of Wine and Roses." Written by J. P. Miller. Aired October 2, 1958, on CBS.

Gould, Jack. "'Patterns' Review." *New York Times*, February 11, 1955.

Gould, Jack. "Prejudice Dissected; Rod Serling's 'A Town Has Turned to Dust' Offered on 'Playhouse 90'." *New York Times*, June 20, 1958.

Grams Jr., Martin. *The Twilight Zone: Unlocking the Door to a Television Classic*. Forest Hill: OTR Publishing, 2008.

Heavey, James. "Angry Young Man? Serling Too Busy." *Sunday Press Writer*, August 15, 1959.

Hughes, James. "Requiem for Rod Serling." *Grantland*, November 19, 2014.

Lacy, Susan, dir. *Rod Serling: Submitted For Your Approval*. 1995; PBS, November 29, 1995. TV Film.

Laven, Arnold, dir. *The United States Steel Hour*. Season 2, Episode 16, "The Rack." Written by Rod Serling. Aired April 12, 1955, on CBS.

Mann, Delbert, dir. *The Philco Television Playhouse*. Season 5, Episode 23, "Marty." Written by Paddy Chayefsky. Aired May 24, 1953, on NBC.

Marschall, Rick. *The Golden Age of Television*. New York: Smithmark, 1995.

Nelson, Ralph, dir. *Playhouse 90*. Season 1, Episode 2, "Requiem for a Heavyweight." Written by Rod Serling. Aired October 11, 1956, on CBS.

Petrie, Daniel, dir. *The United States Steel Hour*. Season 3, Episode 22, "Noon on Doomsday." Written by Rod Serling. Aired April 25, 1956, on CBS.

Sagal, Boris, Steven Spielberg, and Barry Shear, dirs. *Night Gallery*. Written by Rod Serling. 1969; NBC, 1969. TV Film.

Sander, Gordon F. *Serling: The Rise and Twilight of Television's Last Angry Man*. Boston: Dutton Books, 1992.

"Serling Rips TV Censorship." *Binghamton Press & Sun-Bulletin*, May 1, 1964.

Schaffner, Franklin J., dir. *Playhouse 90*. Season 3, Episode 16, "The Velvet Alley." Written by Rod Serling. Aired October 22, 1959, on CBS.

Serling, Rod. *Devils and Demons*. New York: Bantam, 1967.

Serling, Rod. "The Button Pushers." Unpublished radio script, 1951.

Serling, Rod. *The Loner*. Written by Rod Serling. 1965; CBS, September 18, 1965–April 30, 1966. TV Program.

Serling, Rod. *Night Gallery*. Written by Rod Serling. 1970; NBC, 1970–1973. TV Program.

Serling, Rod. *The Season to Be Wary*. New York: Little & Brown, 1967.

Serling, Rod. *The Twilight Zone*. 1959; CBS, October 2, 1959–June 19, 1964. TV Program.

Wallace, Mike. *The Mike Wallace Interview*. "Rod Serling." Conducted by Mike Wallace. Aired September 22, 1959, on ABC.

Webb, Gordon C. "30 Years Later: Rod Serling's Planet of the Apes." *Creative Screenwriting*, 1998.

Reisner, Allen, dir. *Westinghouse Desilu Playhouse*. Season 1, Episode 6, "The Time Element." Written by Rod Serling. Aired November 24, 1958, CBS.

Zicree, Marc Scott. *The Twilight Zone Companion*. Los Angeles: Silman James Press, 1992.